the **VAN DIEMEN**
ANTHOLOGY 2021

THE VAN DIEMEN HISTORY PRIZE

Writing and history have long been lovers, both needing and complementing each other. Non-fiction can make for compelling reading, no matter what the subject, and this is arguably truest when the subject is history. One has only to look at the books – and the sales figures – of Dava Sobel about longitude and Simon Singh about mathematics to see that the work of historians and the art of good writing are natural partners.

It is that collaboration, that love affair, that The Van Diemen History Prize celebrates.

—Chris Champion,
Editor, *Forty South Tasmania* magazine

the VAN DIEMEN ANTHOLOGY 2021

the best of
the VAN DIEMEN HISTORY PRIZE 2020–2021

selected by
Dr Kristyn Harman, Prof Stefan Petrow,
Paige Gleeson and Chris Champion

© 2021
Copyright remains with the individual authors

ISBN 978-0-6452117-6-4

All rights reserved.
Without limiting the rights under copyright above, no part of this publication may be reproduced, stored in or introduced into a retrieval system, or transmitted in any form or by any means (electronic, mechanical, photocopying, recording or otherwise), without the prior written permission of the relevant author.

"The original Franklin-below-Gordon dispute: Beattie, BHP and the Marble Cliffs" by Nic Haygarth has been previously published in *Wonderstruck: Treasuring Tasmania's caves and karst* (Forty South Publishing, 2015).

Published by Forty South Publishing Pty Ltd, Hobart, Tasmania
www.fortysouth.com.au

Printed by IngramSpark

Cover image: Gordon River cruise party.
L. Gray Williams, Weekly Courier, *March 5, 1904, p.23.*

Title page image: Evening, the piner's hut, Gordon River (detail).
Stephen Spurling III, courtesy of Stephen Hiller

CONTENTS

Competition judges vi
Anthology contributors viii

Tony Fenton
    Unsafe harbour 1

Terry Mulhern
    Insubordination and improper intimacy 9

John Beswick
    James Scott: surveyor, explorer and pioneer
    of North-East Tasmania 21

David Faber
    The Goldie incident revisited 30

Madonna Grehan
    Embodied charity in the Maternal and Dorcas Society 40

Nic Haygarth
    The original Franklin-below-Gordon dispute:
    Beattie, BHP and the Marble Cliffs 52

Fiona MacFarlane
    Beware of Mrs Browne 62

Erica Nathan
    The forgotten birdsmith 74

Rohan Price
    The eternal return of Tasmanian trauma 85

Danielle Scrimshaw
    "Fiendish fondness for sin":
    homosexuality and the Tasmanian Gothic 94

Bradley Wood
    The mysterious journey of
    Captain Charles Bayley's scrimshaw cane 103

COMPETITION JUDGES

Dr KRISTYN HARMAN is an Associate Professor in History at the University of Tasmania. Her research interests cohere around socio-cultural frontiers including: transportation to, and within, British colonies; frontier warfare; Indigenous incarceration; and the Australian and New Zealand home fronts during World War II. She is the author of *Cleansing the Colony: Transporting Convicts from New Zealand to Van Diemen's Land* (2017), longlisted for the Royal Society Te Aparangi Award in the Ockham New Zealand Book Awards, 2018. In 2014, Kristyn won the Australian Historical Association Kay Daniels award for her first book, *Aboriginal Convicts: Australian, Khoisan, and Māori Exiles* (2012).

Professor STEFAN PETROW teaches Australian, Tasmanian and European history at the University of Tasmania. His research covers all aspects of Tasmanian history from early settlement to the late twentieth century, but focuses on urban, planning, legal, social and cultural history. He has also published on British, New South Wales, Victorian and Queensland history. His books include *Policing Morals: The Metropolitan Police and the Home Office 1870–1914* (1994), *Going to the Mechanics: The Launceston Mechanics' Institute 1842–1914* (1998) and (with Cary Denholm) *Dr Edward Swarbreck Hall: Colonial Medical Scientist and Moral Activist* (2016). He is currently completing a history of Tasmanian soldiers who served in infantry battalions in World War One called *Tasmanian Anzacs*.

PAIGE GLEESON, a sixth generation Tasmanian and PhD Candidate in History at the University of Tasmania, won the inaugural Van Diemen History Prize in 2018 with her entry, *Fantasy of the Past: Women's History at the Cascade Female Factory*. Paige researches the history of imperial visual culture and museums, and writes about contemporary art and Australian culture. Paige's research interests include feminism and women's history, Indigenous histories of Australia and the Pacific, art in practice and theory, and memory and memorialisation.

CHRIS CHAMPION is editor of *Forty South Tasmania* magazine and a director of Forty South Publishing with responsibility for all editorial functions. He has worked as an editor in Australia and Asia for more than 40 years. The historians on the judging panel assessed all entries and created a short list based on the merit of their historical investigation and writing quality. Chris then chose the winners based on writing quality.

ANTHOLOGY CONTRIBUTORS

TONY FENTON majored in Physics and Computer Science at the University of Tasmania and completed a Graduate Diploma in Information Management. Following a period of work for the State Library of Tasmania, he has devoted most of his time to historical research and writing. His long-standing interest in South West Tasmania – brought about by his grandfather, the legendary tin-miner and naturalist Deny King – led to an exhaustive study of the history of Port Davey. Tony's first book, *A History of Port Davey, Southwest Tasmania, Volume 1: Fleeting hopes* (Forty South Publishing, 2017) was shortlisted in the inaugural Dick and Joan Green Family Award for Tasmanian History in 2018 and longlisted in the 2017 Tasmanian Premier's Literary Prizes, Margaret Scott Prize. A finalist in The Van Diemen History Prize 2018–2019, his essay "Eclipse" was highly commended and appeared in *The Van Diemen Anthology 2019* (Forty South Publishing).

TERRY MULHERN is a writer and biomedical science educator, who works at the University of Melbourne. As a scientist, Terry has published more than 50 research papers in peer-reviewed international journals. But since 2017, he has also written about other things in other places.

Terry was a finalist in The Van Diemen History Prize 2018–2019. His essay "St Valentine's Tears" was highly commended and appeared in *The Van Diemen Anthology 2019* (Forty South Publishing). He has also published in *Forty South Tasmania, The Conversation, Pursuit, Papers and Proceedings of the Royal Society of Tasmania, Science Write Now* and *Australian Biochemist*.

Terry was born in north Queensland, has worked at universities in the UK and around Australia, but his heart is in northwest Tasmania. While Terry has lived in Melbourne for more than 20 years, like a swift parrot he migrates across Bass Strait every summer.

RICHARD JOHN BESWICK (known as John) is a sixth generation Tasmanian. Born at Derby, in the state's North-East, he was educated at Derby State School, Scottsdale and Launceston High Schools and studied later as an external student of the Tasmanian College of Advanced Education. His background in agriculture saw him work, firstly in partnership with his father and then with his wife on the family's 140-hectare dairying property at Derby, during which time he was actively involved in community affairs and served for ten years as a Councillor of the Ringarooma Municipality.

In 1979, he was elected as a Member for Bass in the Tasmanian House of Assembly, a position he held until 1998. From 1982 to 1989, and from 1992 to 1998, he was a cabinet minister in the state government, serving as Deputy Premier of Tasmania from 1992 to 1996. After retiring from Parliament in 1998, he wrote and published his first book, *Brothers' Home: The story of Derby Tasmania* (2003). He has since edited *MacFarlane's History of North-East Tasmania*, (North-Eastern Advertiser, 2007) and written *Tasmania's Forgotten Fontier: A history of exploration, exploitation and settlement around Tasmania's Far North-East Coast* (Forty South Publishing, 2017). He served as a Councillor of the Dorset Council (2009–2014) and as Deputy Mayor (2011–2014).

DAVID FABER (b. Hobart, 1959) is an expatriate Tasmanian labour historian, resident in Adelaide, and Adjunct Research Fellow at Flinders University. Attuned to the historical zeitgeist as an infant covert rebel, he became interested in pirates. This developed at Somerset Primary School into a fascination with wild colonial boys. As an undergraduate at the University of Adelaide, David became aware of the Goldie incident, which occurred on the Cooee foreshore of his alma mater Burnie High School. He recognised the Goldie incident as a "historical event", in E. H. Carr's terminology, attested to by a consensus of historians and exemplifying social situations. He is working on a critical biography of Frank Fantin, the Italian anarchist anti-fascist assassinated on November 16, 1942, at Loveday Internment Camp 14A in South Australia. He speaks Italian.

MADONNA GREHAN is an independent historian, Honorary Fellow at the University of Melbourne's School of Health Sciences and a Registered General Nurse and Midwife. Her research interests centre on the history of nursing and midwifery in Australia since 1790, oral history, social history, biography and material culture.

Dr Grehan held the C. J. La Trobe Society Fellowship at State Library of Victoria in 2013 and the John Oxley Library Fellowship at State Library of Queensland in 2015. She was awarded the Silver Medal of the Centaur Memorial Fund for Nurses in 2018, for promoting and honouring the memory of the 2/3 Australian Hospital Ship *Centaur*. Dr Grehan is immediate Past President of the Australian and New Zealand Society of the History of Medicine, and member of a human research ethics committee at the University of Melbourne.

NIC HAYGARTH is a professional historian and freelance writer who was awarded a PhD in History by the University of Tasmania. A prolific author, his most recent publications include *Mountain Men: Stories from the Tasmanian High Country* (with Simon Cubit, 2015), *Wonderstruck: Treasuring Tasmania's caves and karst* (2015) and *On the Ossie: Tasmanian osmiridium and the fountain pen industry* (2017) – all published by Forty South Publishing. Nic is particularly passionate about Tasmania's wild places, high country and those who populate such areas. Nic was a finalist in The Van Diemen History Prize 2018–2019 with his essay "The passing of the 'tigerman'".

FIONA MacFARLANE is a retired Hobart-based archivist, with twenty years of archival and historical research experience, gained primarily through working with the Tasmanian Archive and Heritage Office (TAHO, part of Libraries Tasmania). She now works as a freelance Tasmanian historical researcher, working for renowned University of Sydney writer and academic, Professor Cassandra Pybus. In Fiona's spare time she enjoys transcribing diaries that were written by women living in Hobart in the mid nineteenth century and has self-published several fiction and non-fiction books including *Breakfast at Midnight* and *Quirky Names in Tasmanian History*. She has recently transcribed Harriet Gore Browne's diaries and hopes to publish these in 2021.

ERICA NATHAN has published academic work as an environmental historian, including her history of the Moorabool, *Lost Waters*, while her more general writing has appeared in journals such as *Forty South Tasmania* and *Meanjin*. She was shortlisted for the Nature Conservancy (Australia) Nature Writing prize with her *Heard Island Is a Place*. She gardens alongside native birds, ambles through Hobart's Domain, and ventures into the wider island tracking rivers and imagining past landscapes.

ROHAN PRICE authors books on the role of violence and nationalism on the policies of the British Far East. He specialises in the influence of property law and compensation policy on civic identity in the old British colonies and the use of social welfare in the decolonisation of Asian colonies. His most recent work applies interpretive approaches drawn from Nietzsche to South East Asian contexts.

Rohan's publications include the acclaimed *Going Native: The passions of Philip Jacks* (2016, Australian Scholarly) and *Reading Colonies: Property and control of the British Far East* (2016, City University Press of HK). In 2019, he published *Resistance in Colonial and Communist China (1950–1963): Anatomy of a riot* for Routledge History. His most recent work, *Violence and Emancipation in Colonial Ideology: Hong Kong and British Malaya* has been called "a major contribution to the literature" holding "an unparalleled command of both scholarly literature and primary sources".

Rohan is working on two new manuscripts under contract: "Nietzsche, Heidegger and Colonialism: Occupying South East Asia" (Routledge Studies in History) and "Nietzsche and Colonial Nostalgia" (Peter Lang Prompts). In 2020 he published a co-edited a book, *Regulatory Issues in Organic Food Safety in the Asia Pacific*.

Rohan is well known nationally for his text *Principles of Employment Law* which has reached its 5th edition.

DANIELLE SCRIMSHAW is a recent graduate of the University of Melbourne and writer of fiction, memoir, and creative nonfiction. Her Honours research, supervised by Joy Damousi, focused on Australian women's queer sexualities and the contexts in which they were contained from the 1840s to the 1920s. She has written for *Voiceworks, Overland, Archer* and *Scum Mag*.

BRADLEY WOOD has always had a passion for history. Since fleeing the mainland for Tasmania six years ago as a climate change refugee, he has worked on archaeological excavations, visited historical sites, and trawled Tasmanian archival material. He believes that to appreciate our present world we need to know and retell the stories of our past.

JOINT WINNER, THE VAN DIEMEN HISTORY PRIZE 2020-2021

Unsafe harbour
TONY FENTON

Two fishing boats ply the south coast of Tasmania, as they have done countless times before – but this time is different. In February 1933, strong gales buffet the island, catching the crews of *Corona* and *Doris Jane* away from port. The fishermen dash for New Harbour, a small bay open to the south with a few rocks at the entrance affording scant protection. They are tossed about for an entire fortnight in this anchorage, knowing all this time that a slight change in the wind means shipwreck.[1]

Friends and family of the crew had no way of knowing if their loved ones were safe – marine radio was a new technology out of reach for owners of such small vessels. Communications with Maatsuyker Island lighthouse revealed that the boats had been spotted on February 24 in Cox Bight. The lightkeeper thought they would probably have sheltered in nearby New Harbour, but couldn't be certain. The news did little to allay people's fears.[2]

Lobbying from Southport residents prompted the government to arrange a search. Sergeant Tom Challenger of the Water Police was to venture forth in the Sea Fisheries Board's patrol boat *Allara*. Conditions were so poor that even the passage from Hobart to Recherche Bay was uncomfortably rough. Simultaneously, arrangements were made for a seaplane from HMAS *Albatross* (then at anchor in North West Bay) to make a reconnaissance.[3] *Albatross* steamed to Southport and launched a seaplane at first light on March 2. The crew sighted two boats at anchor in New Harbour, and men waved to the plane from the beach. The aviators had intended to drop message bags, but conditions proved too rough. Seeing that the fishermen were safe, *Allara* was recalled and the search called off.[4]

Although exposed to the wrath of the elements from the south, New Harbour is the only shelter between Recherche Bay in the east and Port Davey in the west. For fishermen working the south-western coast in boats so much smaller and lower powered than they are today, Recherche was too far if the weather changed suddenly. To reach Port Davey, on the other hand, meant rounding the notorious South West Cape while beating into the prevailing north-westerly winds. This is the story of a struggle to ameliorate the dangers faced by the coastal fishing fleet.

The 1933 incident precipitated calls for moorings to be laid in New Harbour to give vessels a better chance of riding out storms. The Sea Fisheries Board concurred with the fishermen, while the Hobart Marine Board wanted nothing to do with it, a position for which it was roundly criticised. The marine board objected that if it were to place a mooring in New Harbour, fishermen in other localities would be justified in asking for moorings too. The board was, however, willing to donate a spare buoy for the scheme on the condition that they "accept no responsibility in any direction whatever".[5]

Arthur Stubbings, a tin miner who relied on south-coast fishermen for transport of supplies to and ore from his mine, declared that the marine board wardens had no idea what they were talking about and should swap places with the fishermen.[6]

Thanks in part to the efforts of John Dwyer, MHA, a mooring was put down a year later, and the matter was seemingly laid to rest. However, in 1935 another incident brought the issue to the fore again. The McKay brothers, of the fishing boat *Ronena,* had seen another boat, *Galena,* fishing off New Harbour and expected her to return. She was worked single-handedly by 65-year-old Alex Hutchings, who had been badly injured in a logging accident a year before. The McKays became increasingly worried when *Galena* did not show up, and at length went out in search. Travelling east, they found nothing until reaching Louisa Island, where they came across some spars, a portion of a deck and part of a dinghy, forlornly floating in the sea. They continued the search but found nothing further, and no trace of Hutchings.

Ronena then went to Port Davey where the McKays continued their fishing. There they came across the yacht *Conella,* told her crew the news and, since they were about to return to Hobart, asked them to report the tragedy to the police. This they did, and the newspapers covered the story. As the days went past, the public learnt more details that made Hutchings' survival seem increasingly unlikely. The boat's engine had "gone bung", said one fisherman,

New Harbour.
Photograph Geoff Fenton

and Hutchings had had only four days' food left. Challenger knew that the missing man had poor eyesight, and *Galena* was not in a condition to withstand the heavy weather that had buffeted the coast.

Three days after news of the wreck had reached Hobart, the public was relieved to learn that Hutchings was safe. He had been fishing near Louisa Island when his boat struck a rock during a fog. Fortunately he was able to wade ashore. Apparently unscathed, he made his way to where another boat was lying, and worked aboard that vessel until the skipper was ready to return to town.

Although this drama occurred some 20 kilometres east of New Harbour, it galvanised the lobbying for shelter for fishermen. A year later, three half-ton concrete blocks were laid down as moorings in New Harbour. Now fishermen could pick up the attached buoy and rope, and ride out bad weather much more safely than they could with their own anchors.

So it was hoped. But in a storm four years later the moorings were found inadequate. A "terrific storm" hit the coast one winter, catching out three fishing boats, including *Lurline* and *Seafarer*. Even with the boats' anchors down, the mooring weights dragged along the sea bed and *Lurline* passed the other vessel.

L. Mazey, on *Lurline,* ran his engine at full power. Even so, the vessel dragged, narrowly missing a rocky point and shipwreck. He let out another anchor, but now *Seafarer* bore down on *Lurline* and collided. She became entangled in *Lurline*'s lines. For half an hour her stern thrashed *Lurline*'s bow. In this melee, *Seafarer*'s rudder and mizzen rigging were damaged, while Lurline's bow was smashed in.

After much effort, *Seafarer*'s crew managed to get a line ashore and pull clear of *Lurline*. Mazey and his mate Garrett feared their vessel would go to the bottom. They set out for shore in a dinghy. Huge surf dashed the dinghy onto the rocks, capsizing and damaging it. The men managed to haul it to safety. There they remained ashore until, during the night, the storm abated. The battered vessels limped back to civilisation shortly afterwards.[7]

The moorings had proven inadequate and Challenger criticised their position, saying that the windward vessel could foul the others if it dragged, as had been demonstrated by *Lurline* and *Seafarer*. Several people suggested that ships' anchors or mushroom-shaped anchors constructed from condemned boiler ends would hold much better in the sandy bottom of New Harbour. At length the Sea Fisheries Board decided to lay ships' anchors, and by July 1939 three anchors weighing one or two tons each were in position.[8]

The moorings were now safe, but big swells from the south could still toss sheltering boats like bath toys. The Sea Fisheries Board had earlier proposed constructing breakwaters at New Harbour and at Boat Harbour on the east coast using Commonwealth funding then available for unemployment relief projects aimed at developing fisheries. Alas, a reduction in the Commonwealth loan quota meant that funding was not forthcoming.[9] The board remained interested in the idea of a breakwater to protect the tenuous anchorage, but for now it had to confine itself to providing moorings.[10]

The Hobart Marine Board's concern that placing moorings at New Harbour would lead to a flood of requests for similar works elsewhere proved well founded. Fishermen began to call for moorings, breakwaters and lighthouses all around the state. But the Department of Agriculture (which had absorbed the Sea Fisheries Board) was more receptive to fishermen's suggestions. It saw such developments as a means of opening up more remote fishing grounds and taking pressure off those closer to populated areas, which even then were becoming depleted.[11]

A fourth mooring was laid in 1941, and maintenance was delegated to south-coast fishing identity Syd Dale. He periodically checked and repaired the moorings as needed throughout the 1940s free of charge. All that the Sea Fisheries Board (and later the Department of Agriculture) had to provide was materials. Typically, a maintenance inventory would consist of so many fathoms of chain and manila rope, so many glass buoys, and perhaps antifouling paint.[12] It was not just nature that took a toll on the moorings: suspicions arose that the buoys and even ropes were pilfered, either exchanged with inferior ones, or the chains simply allowed to sink.[13]

This state of affairs remained throughout the war years. Then in 1950 Dale was unable to locate the moorings after the buoys had once again disappeared. This was to have near-fatal consequences a year-and-a-half later.

Dale's son Colin, on *Denalis,* and stepson Clyde Clayton, on *Arlie D,* anchored in New Harbour that fateful October. The sea was as "calm as grease" – too calm, felt Clyde's wife and deckhand Win. Colin and Clyde took advantage of the calm conditions to go ashore and gather firewood. In the small hours of the morning a change in the boat's movement woke Win. An hour later the storm hit, a south-easter with waves breaking across the mouth of the bay. As the day wore on, the gale increased its fury, huge breakers sending spray hurtling over the 16-metre high inner rocks.

The undertow current forced the boats' vulnerable sterns toward the oncoming waves, which threatened to crash over them. The skippers had to use their engines to prevent the anchor chains suddenly snatching and possibly breaking, requiring them to constantly adjust throttle and helm. With breakers alarmingly close behind, *Arlie D* had to move further out. In this perilous situation Clyde was unable to leave the helm to help Win raise the anchor. So Colin transferred his deckhand brother Trevor Dale to the dinghy and let him back astern on a long line. Win and Trevor battled with the anchor as Clyde struggled to keep *Arlie D* pointing into the wind.

Thanks to the more powerful and reliable post-war engines, *Arlie D* could move away from the snarling rocks. But soon she dragged back toward *Denalis*. There was nothing to do but keep the boats apart using their engines. In this position they kept vigil for 12 long hours. Although tossed by giant swells, they were in the only part of the bay that wasn't breaking.

By late afternoon the sea began to break over the boats. It was time to abandon ship. Colin and Clyde expertly brought their dinghies ashore through ferocious surf and somehow landed them safely on the rocks. Once ashore they overturned the dinghies and lashed them down securely. After this ordeal they clambered to a small sea cave to spend a miserable night, though a fire and a cup of tea provided some small comfort. At the peak of the storm the sea threatened to flood the cave, adding to the castaways' alarm.

The four crew fully expected next morning to find their boats reduced to matchsticks. So they were amazed and relieved when, peering out at daylight, they saw two "sturdy ships rocking bravely on their anchors". In the calm after the storm, they retrieved a drum of diesel which had broken free from its lashings on the deck of *Denalis* and washed ashore. Then it was back aboard their vessels to make things ship-shape.

■

Tin miner Deny King, concerned that fishing boats may have come to grief in the storm, made the four-hour trek to New Harbour from Melaleuca, and was perturbed to find that his sister Win had had such a close call.[14]

This narrow scrape prompted the fisheries division of the Department of Agriculture to once more have the moorings renewed. Two years later it went further, at last acting on long-called-for breakwaters at anchorages frequented by fishermen. The simplest solution was to sink a large ship in shallow water to seaward of the moorings, and this method was used at New Harbour and at Walkers Corner in Fortescue Bay.

For the New Harbour breakwater, the Minister for Agriculture approached the Union Steamship Company of New Zealand (USSNZ) offering to buy their coal hulk *Jessie Craig* for a nominal sum.[15] *Jessie Craig* was a 55-metre iron barque built in Scotland as *Isola* in 1876. Trading first out of Denmark, after 20 years she was bought by the Auckland-based Craig Line for use on the Australia-New Zealand service which she plied until being reduced to a floating coal store at Hobart in 1914.[16]

The USSNZ company let the department have the hulk free of charge after stripping her of valuable machinery.[17] The fisheries division then contracted George Cheverton to fill the vessel with more than 100 tons of gravel and sand for ballast. After clearing the way with various other government departments (even the marine board did not object, provided holes were made in her to ensure she would not float away), all was ready.

On May 5, 1953, the once-proud barque was towed out of Hobart by the tugboat *Boyer*, and proceeded on her final voyage in company with the fisheries trawler *Liawenee* (whose master was none other than Syd Dale). All went smoothly at first. Then, while manoeuvring *Jessie Craig* into position, the towing lines snapped under the enormous strain, increased by the surging

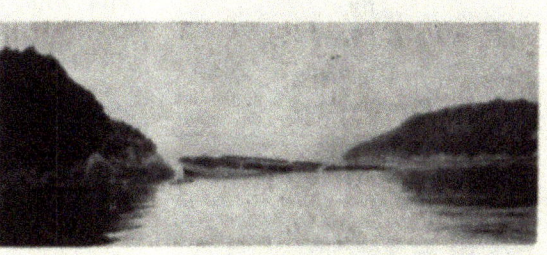

An article from *Fisheries Newsletter*, July 1953, of the Tasmanian Department of Commerce and Agriculture, showing a photograph of the *Jessie Craig* in position.
Courtesy of the National Library of Australia

waters. At last in position, holes were blasted in the hulk, which settled firmly on the sandy bottom.[18]

John Dwyer, now the Minister for Fisheries, who had been aboard *Liawenee* "supervising" the operation, confidently predicted that the breakwater would shelter fishermen for the next 20 or 30 years. Yet a fisherman reported that within a week a moderate gale blew up and the seaward side of the hulk stove in. He maintained that few fishermen had been consulted about the breakwater, and as a result it had been placed in the wrong position.[19] Other rumours circulated that the team had been over-generous with the gelignite. Either way, the breakwater soon broke up.[20]

In addition to the breakwater, another mooring was laid using one of *Jessie Craig*'s anchors. The cycle of renewing sunken moorings continued throughout the 1950s, but by the end of the decade the fisheries division had had enough, and there is no evidence that the moorings were renewed after that date.

Four years later Des Whayman called for improvements to New Harbour after he rescued crew from the doomed fishing boat *Leanne* in mountainous seas among the Maatsuyker Islands. He contended that by excavating material from a nearby hill, a suitable breakwater could be constructed. Although Rupert Brown MLC supported Whayman's views, nothing further was done.[21]

With the availability of marine radio, reliable engines and better forecasting, the need for moorings in remote places has slowly diminished, and today the struggle to provide safe harbours for fishermen has become just another turbulent backwater of Tasmanian history.

■ ■ ■

ENDNOTES

1. *Mercury*, March 8, 1933: 8.
2. *Mercury*, February 27, 1933: 3.
3. *Mercury*, March 2, 1933: 7.
4. *Mercury*, March 3, 1933: 7.
5. Minutes of the Marine Board of Hobart, June 27, 1933, TAHO: AB830/1/14.
6. *Mercury*, April 22, 1933: 8.
7. *Mercury*, June 27, 1938: 2.
8. *Mercury*, July 20, 1938: 7; *Mercury*, July 6, 1939: 3.
9. *Mercury*, May 16, 1936: 16.
10. Sea Fisheries Board of Tasmania, *Report of the Board for the Years 1933–1939* (Tasmania: the board, 1940).
11. D'Alton to Martyn, October 23, 1941, AA816/1/2 file 18/4A (Tasmanian Archive and Heritage Office, hereafter TAHO).
12. E. Parkes to Syd Dale, October 8, 1942, AA816/1/3 file 18/4 (TAHO).
13. Janet Fenton, *Win & Clyde: Side by side in Tasmania's far South West* (Hobart: Forty Degrees South, 2010), 155; *Mercury*, 12 November 1963.
14. Ibid., 150–154.
15. Graeme Broxam and Michael Nash, *Tasmanian Shipwrecks: Volume 2 1900–2012* (Hobart: Navarine, 2013), 264, 280; AD9/1/20734 (TAHO), passim.
16. *Mercury*, April 22, 1953: 12.
17. Captain Grace to Dwyer, March 19, 1953, AD9/1/20734 (TAHO).
18. AD9/1/20734 (TAHO), passim.
19. *Examiner*, June 5, 1953: 6.
20. Janet Fenton, *Win & Clyde*: 155.
21. AD9/1/20734 (TAHO), passim.

JOINT WINNER, THE VAN DIEMEN HISTORY PRIZE 2020-2021

Insubordination and improper intimacy

Sex, violence and mutiny aboard the *Cape Packet*

TERRY MULHERN

Saturday, October 1, 1825, dawned bleak and blustery in the port of Cowes on the Isle of Wight. Two weeks earlier, Captain William Kellie, of the *Cape Packet*, had loaded his cargo at the London docks. Contrary winds made it hard going and it took Kellie 11 days to sail 220 miles to Cowes. Here, he picked up livestock and passengers.

Most had already boarded when one gentleman claimed his wife was too ill to embark. But time and tide wait for no man – or his wife. This morning, the tide was right, and the wind had veered a point in Kellie's favour. He ordered his first mate, William Ruxton, to weigh anchor and make sail.

As the ship rounded the point and passed Hurst Castle, the three tall rock stacks of the Needles came into view. But not for long. The ship now met the full force of the wind, heavy seas and sheets of torrential rain. In Kellie's haste, many items of cargo, as well as live animals, were yet to be stowed. Boxes slewed across the streaming decks and two frightened pigs were washed overboard. While the crew scrambled to make things fast, the drenched, seasick passengers retreated below.

All day, Kellie tacked back and forth, making little headway while the gale increased. Begrudgingly, he turned back to Cowes, coming to anchor at midnight. One of the passengers, Henry Hellyer, wrote, "It was mortifying

Henry Hellyer's sketches of life aboard the *Cape Packet*.[1]
"A Deck Scene" depicts the ship battling the gale in the English Channel on October 1, 1825. The "two frightened pigs" washed overboard are shown tumbling across the deck. "A Cuddy Scene" shows the passengers in the cuddy – an enclosed space under the fore part of the poop (rear) deck which was used as the dining room for the ship's officers and passengers.

From Voyage to Van Diemen's Land, *reproduced with the permission of the Tasmanian Archive and Heritage Office* to find we had endured all this and might as well have remained quietly at Cowes".[2] But there was a silver lining. With an extra day's grace, the gentleman's wife recovered sufficiently to board. Another 11 days passed, including a further failed attempt to depart, before finally, on Wednesday, October 12, the *Cape Packet* embarked on her long voyage to Van Diemen's Land.

■

The *Cape Packet* was a 250-ton brig. Her crew consisted of the captain, his two mates and 20 seamen. She may have been small, barely 100 feet long and 25 feet wide, but what she lacked in size, she made up for in speed and manoeuvrability. And she had teeth. On her deck were four twelve-pounders and below was an armoury packed with small arms and cutlasses.[3] The threat of piracy was real, and she would have made a stunning prize. The *Cape Packet* was conveying valuable commodities to the Australian colonies, including 100 hogsheads of beer, two brewing coppers, iron bar, sheet lead, mill stones and canvas.

But that's not all. She also carried treasure: 20 boxes of Spanish dollars, worth £20,000 then and millions today.[4] This was the capital with which Hellyer's employers, the Van Diemen's Land Company, would establish the first white settlement in north-west Tasmania,[5] the remotest corner of the remotest colony in the British Empire.

Also aboard were 17 passengers, composed of VDL Co "officers", their families and servants.[6] Their leader was Edward Curr Esquire, the company's local agent. Curr was accompanied by his wife Elizabeth (née Micklethwaite) and their three boys, Edward, William and Richard, all under the age of five.

Curr's second-in-command was Stephen Adey, the company's superintendent of lands. With him was his bride Lucy (née Rede). They had been married just two months. Also travelling with the Adeys was Lucy's widowed sister, Mary Grimstone.[7] It is unlikely Lucy would have agreed to travel halfway around the world without her older sister. It was Lucy's ill health that had caused the Adeys to miss that first aborted departure, a fact neither Lucy nor Mary mentioned in their farewell letters posted from Cowes, lest it cause even further distress for their mother.[8]

The other company officers were Alexander Goldie – agriculturalist, Henry Hellyer – chief surveyor and architect; and two junior surveyors, Clement Lorymer and Joseph Fossey. The remaining five passengers were servants, including two young women – maids of the senior officers' wives.

Due to inclement weather, the passengers spent their first days at sea in the ship's cuddy, which served as both dining and drawing room.[9] The ship's galley and the cuddy's wine bin were well-stocked, and Captain Kellie appeared both charming and thoughtful, telling the ladies they may "send to the steward at any time for whatever we thought proper".[10]

While the gentlemen smoked, the ladies played chess. Conversation was lively and good-natured. Hellyer found a kindred spirit in Mary Grimstone. They discussed their shared love of art, literature and theatre. Mary was a published poet and novelist[11] and Hellyer told her of his dream to publish his journal, in which he would chronicle their *Voyage to Van Diemen's Land*.[12]

As they made their way south, the weather improved. In less than two weeks, they reached their first port of call, the exotic Portuguese island of Madeira, 400 miles off Morocco. While the ship took on fresh water and provisions, the passengers enjoyed an afternoon ashore. They wandered Funchal's streets and markets, tasting delicious tropical fruit and sampling the local wines. They "saw no wheeled carriages of any description" on the steep cobbled streets, but instead "sledges drawn by little bullocks about the size of donkies".[13] Tired but exhilarated, the passengers reboarded and bid a fond adieu to Funchal, as the *Cape Packet* sailed out of the harbour at sunset.

In the cuddy, oranges and lemons hung from the ceiling. On deck, the ship's boats were filled with bananas and the stern festooned with slings of grapes, which "made the ship look like a fruiterer's shop".[14] With each passing day, more and more time was spent on deck to escape the heat below. On October 27, the wind died, and the ship was becalmed. The sun beat mercilessly upon the white deck, the glare painful to the eye. A canvas awning was rigged up to provide shade.[15]

∎

The *Cape Packet* crossed the Tropic of Cancer on October 30. Hellyer noted they had entered the "Torrid Zone".[16] In the steaming cuddy, sharp words were exchanged over trifling differences. An argument broke out among the servants over the rationing of fresh water. On November 5, Hellyer noted "a deadly silence pervaded the company all the evening... I retired to my oven much vexed to see such disagreements between the captain and our party, particularly as it was about nothing but an angry word".[17]

Hellyer was mistaken. It was due to more than just "an angry word". The Adeys' pretty maid Gwen had caught the eye of Captain Kellie. When

A view of Funchal in Madeira, Portugal by Henry Hellyer.[18]
Hellyer shows the *Cape Packet* in the foreground. The two little rowing boats in the centre have raised curved prows of the local "fashion".
From Voyage to Van Diemen's Land, *reproduced with the permission of the Tasmanian Archive and Heritage Office*

she rebuffed his advances, Kellie spread innuendo about her with the crew and rumours among the servants that Gwen was disrespectful towards her employers. Lucy Adey sensed something was amiss and interrogated a tearful Gwen to discover the truth. Stephen Adey was incensed a trusted family servant had been so mistreated and maligned by Kellie.[19]

The Captain was in conference with first mate Ruxton when Adey found him. Kellie was taken aback by Adey's onslaught. When Ruxton supported Adey, instead of his Captain, an incredulous Kellie dismissed him on the spot, sowing bitter seeds that would be reaped later in the voyage. Backed into a corner, Kellie decided attack was the best form of defence. In a booming voice, so all on deck would hear, he accused Adey of "improper intimacy" with his wife's maid. Adey "told him he was a liar".[20] With his honour as a gentleman at stake, there was talk of a duel. A "distressed & agitated" Adey summoned Curr to his cabin. With Lucy at his side, Adey laid the sordid details of the captain's behaviour before his superior. Lucy later wrote glowingly of Curr's unstinting support for Adey. From this day forth, Lucy and her sister Mary refused to speak a word to the captain.[21]

In return, Kellie made his passengers as uncomfortable as possible. Whether by design or coincidence, a dreadful stench rose from the bilge and pervaded the ship. The "unwholesome effluvia" left the passengers gagging and their cabin walls streaked with black.[22] Curr demanded something be done. Kellie refused. When Curr pushed the matter, Kellie responded, "I won't do it and that's flat."[23]

Three days later, even Kellie could stand the smell no longer. The ships pumps were inspected and found to be clogged with gravel. It took two days to clear them, then all hands, including Hellyer and the other surveyors, worked the pumps all day in shifts to flush the stinking bilge water from the ship.[24]

■

Saturday, November 26 began much like any other long hot day aboard the *Cape Packet*. The gentlemen fished while the ladies sat in the shade of the awning. The Curr boys watched sailors take turns hurling the "grains", a five-pronged fishing spear with a line at the end,[25] at the large bonito and albacore "sporting and leaping before the Ship's Bows".[26] Captain Kellie stood aloof on his quarterdeck. At midday, dinner was served in the "melting hot" cuddy, after which everyone returned on deck.[27]

Later, Curr noticed the captain absent from his usual station. Suspicious, he quietly descended the stairs to the cabins. At the bottom, he found himself face-to-face with a surprised Kellie. Over the captain's shoulder, Curr saw movement in his own cabin's doorway. His suspicions were confirmed. Kellie had turned his amorous attentions to Elizabeth Curr's 19-year-old maid, Mary Wogan.

Never one to mince his words, Curr accused the captain of having "seduced" his servant.[28] An indignant Kellie, almost literally caught with his pants down, pushed past Curr, saying he would not be insulted in his own vessel. On the quarterdeck the two angry men stood toe-to-toe. Curr hissed, "I think sir, that 'tis I that am insulted."[29]

Kellie ordered Curr from the quarterdeck, and when Curr refused, Kellie threatened to use force. The six-foot, tall broad-shouldered Yorkshireman stared down the captain and replied, "Then you may force me, for I won't stir."[30] By this time, all passengers and crew were on deck watching the unfolding drama. The Captain ordered the second mate and two sailors to man-handle Curr off the quarterdeck and barked for his pistols to be loaded and brought to him.

Armed, and once more in sole control of his quarterdeck, Kellie addressed the crew. "My men, there's a conspiracy on board amongst the passengers. I have been insulted on my quarterdeck. This ship contains specie [coin] and a valuable cargo. What their motive is I do not know. It may be to take the ship and I call upon you all to attend to my orders and report to me every circumstance that comes under your observation – and the first nan who disobeys my orders, I will blow his brains out!"[31]

Mary Grimstone, never one to take a backward step, pushed to the front and regaled the crew, "Take the ship! And make me captain." Kellie sneered, "A lady's impertinence is too contemptible to be noticed."[32] He ordered the passengers locked in their cabins and posted armed sentries. Hellyer's entry for this extraordinary day finished with the words, "We all wished we had got to Rio, and were determined to proceed no farther than that on this ship."[33]

Next morning, Curr assembled his officers. He'd regained his composure and resolved to "remain quiet, till we get to Rio".[34] Captain Kellie, on the other hand, continued to vent his rage. Mary Wogan's relationship with the Curr family was at an end. Curr told her, "You are going to the gallows as fast as you can", to which she retorted, "No Sir, I am going to Botany Bay,"[35] – meaning, after they reached Hobart, she would continue with Kellie to Sydney. Mary was no longer Curr's servant. She'd moved into the Captain's cabin and was now Kellie's mistress.[36]

The lights of Rio came into view on the night of December 3. Inexplicably, Hellyer's journal ends abruptly, mid-page.[37] Curr, aware of Hellyer's desire to publish the tale of the *Cape Packet*'s voyage, must have insisted the company's dirty laundry not be aired this way. But Curr had less power over Lucy Adey and Mary Grimstone. Their letters home from Rio described the scandal in detail.

Then, in a startling about-turn, the passengers agreed to continue onboard the *Cape Packet*. Lucy Adey wrote this footnote, before sealing her letter.

> Dec.ʳ 7ᵗʰ 1825
> The Captⁿ Mr Adey & Mr Curr have been before the British Counsel here, & a mutual reconciliation has taken place. The Captⁿ has pledged himself to the Counsel to do all in his power to make us comfortable and we shall sail again on Sunday. I suppose we shall be in V. D. Land early in February. Godbless you all write fully & as soon as possible.[38]

A page from Lucy Adey and Mary Grimstone's letter home from Rio de Janiero, December 1825.[39] This is the "envelope" which was simply a page of paper wrapped around the other folded pages then sealed. Postage was expensive, so no paper was wasted and the letter was written "crossed" with lines running horizontal and vertical – even on the envelope's concealed flaps.

Reproduced with the permission of the Beinecke Rare Book and Manuscript Library, Yale University

■

Twelve weeks later, the *Cape Packet* reached Hobart Town. The run across the South Atlantic must have been good, as they didn't stop to take on water at Cape Town.[40]

But what happened after the *Cape Packet* entered the vastness of the Indian Ocean?

According to newspaper reports of the trial of Captain William Kellie, the uneasy truce lasted no more than six weeks.[41] On January 24, in the middle of the Indian Ocean, the ship was again becalmed. With the captain in his cabin, perhaps explaining the finer points of celestial navigation to Mary Wogan, Adey and Ruxton decided it would be fine sport to shoot seabirds. With Goldie and two sailors, they lowered a ship's boat and rowed away from the *Cape Packet*.

When Kellie heard shots, he burst from his cabin and hurried on deck. He fired a musket and signaled for the boat's return. When they didn't respond, Kellie fired several more times. He maintained it was simply to gain their attention, but those in the boat disagreed. When they came alongside, a furious Kellie said, "If they had not returned, he should have fired a carronade into the boat and sunk them."[42] Adey was livid, claiming to have felt the wind of a musket ball.

Three weeks later, Ruxton and the captain clashed violently. The mate was clapped in irons. The mood aboard was black, and the crew's allegiance split. During the night, someone freed Ruxton by filing through his handcuffs. An enraged Kellie assembled the crew. Again brandishing pistols, he demanded to know who the culprits were. He was met with stony silence. Kellie ordered the ship's carpenter John Sales to put new irons on Ruxton. When the crew blocked Sale's way, Kellie warned them, "The first man that interferes, I will blow his brains out." Seaman Valentine Hobbs spoke up, "Let Mr Ruxton be under a bond, and if he breaks that, do as you will with him." The Captain's eyes narrowed, "Out of this, every one of you," and to the carpenter, "You hold him and I will put them on myself."[43]

With Ruxton in chains, Kellie went in search of Hobbs, who was in the galley lighting his pipe. Two starkly contrasting versions were presented of what happened next. Hobbs claimed Kellie looked in from the forecastle, got down on one knee, took aim and fired. The ball struck Hobbs' left side but deflected from a rib and left him with a superficial wound the size of "a crown piece". Under oath, John Sales gave a different account. He said the captain had only "entreated the men in a mild way" and there was "a great scuffle in the forecastle, and that the pistol, when raised, went off".[44]

■

The week of the *Cape Packet*'s arrival in Hobart was a busy one for the Magistrates Court. It sat from Monday to Saturday dealing with Kellie, his crew and passengers. Kellie charged the crew with "extreme insubordination, amounting to mutiny".[45] Hobbs countered, seeking a warrant against Kellie for attempted murder. Then Adey joined the fray. There was much legal argument over whether mutiny even existed as a crime on a merchant vessel (it didn't) and whether Kellie was accused of capital offences. To Adey's disgust, his charge against Kellie was dismissed.[46] In the end, only Hobbs' complaint was pursued. Kellie was committed for trial for "malicious shooting with intent to kill on the high seas".[47]

A month later in the Supreme Court, Adey, Curr, Lorymer, Fossey and half the crew gave evidence for the prosecution. The defense called John Sales, re-examined Fossey and heard from the defendant.[48] The trial lasted three days, often sitting late into the night. In summing up, Chief Justice Pedder told the jury, "Captains of merchant vessels, like other persons in situations of authority, have certain powers entrusted to them ... and might, by reasonable means enforce them." The jury of six was composed entirely of serving or retired military officers. It took them "only a few minutes" to return a verdict of not guilty.[49]

The whole affair was an embarrassment for the company and its officers, but they did manage to keep the voyage's more scandalous details quiet. While Adey still bore a grudge,[50] Curr was congratulated by the company directors for having "sacrificed your private feelings to the good of the Company".[51]

Kellie may have been a free man, but no sailor in Hobart would sign on with the clearly "mad, bad and dangerous" Captain Kellie. With half a cargo still to be delivered to Sydney, Kellie swallowed his pride. To placate the crew, a local sailing master, John Laughton, was engaged to command the *Cape Packet* on the last leg of its journey.[52] Once in Sydney, and paid, Ruxton, Hobbs and the other "mutineers" abandoned ship for good. Kellie retook command, hired new crew and returned to England.[53]

The *Cape Packet* returned to Australasian waters in 1830, this time fitted out as a whaler – but without Kellie.[54] After his return to England, Kellie seems to have vanished without a trace. It can only be hoped he was never again entrusted with the lives of crew and passengers. The sordid tale of the voyage of the *Cape Packet* begs the question, how on earth did the Van Diemen's Land Company directors ever come to enlist the services of a man with such a flawed character and so unfit for command as Captain William Kellie.

■ ■ ■

ENDNOTES

1. Henry Hellyer, *Voyage to Van Diemen's Land* (Original illustrated manuscript, 1825, TAHO NS433/1/2), 1. https://stors.tas.gov.au/NS433-1-2$init=NS433-1-2P00.
2. Ibid., 1.
3. *Hobart Town Gazette*, Shipping Intelligence, Saturday, March 11, 1826, 2.

4. James Bischoff, *Sketch of the History of Van Diemen's Land, illustrated by a map of the island and an account of the Van Diemen's Land Company* (London: John Richardson, Royal Exchange, 1832).
5. Hellyer, *Voyage to Van Diemen's Land*, 1.
6. Michael Roe, "Mary Leman Grimstone (1800–1850?): For Women's Rights and Tasmanian Patriotism." *Papers and Proceedings: Tasmanian Historical Research Association*, 36, No. 1, (1989): 8–32; and: Michael Roe, "Yet More About Mary Leman Grimstone." *Papers and Proceedings: Tasmanian Historical Research Association*, 59, No. 3, (2012): 189–193.
7. Mary Leman Grimstone, *Scrapbook* (Beinecke Rare Book and Manuscript Library: Original Manuscript, 1832 [begun]), 48a–b. https://brbl-dl.library.yale.edu/vufind/Record/3600379.
8. Hellyer, *Voyage to Van Diemen's Land*, 2.
9. Mary Leman Grimstone, *Scrapbook*, 49a.
10. Michael Roe, "Mary Leman Grimstone,", 8–32.
11. Hellyer, *Voyage to Van Diemen's Land*, 1–31.
12. Ibid., 9–14.
13. Ibid., 14.
14. Ibid., 15.
15. Ibid., 16.
16. Ibid., 18.
17. Mary Leman Grimstone, *Scrapbook*, 49a.
18. Ibid.
19. Ibid., 49b.
20. Hellyer, *Voyage to Van Diemen's Land*, 21.
21. Mary Leman Grimstone, *Scrapbook*, 49b.
22. Hellyer, *Voyage to Van Diemen's Land*, 21.
23. William Henry Smyth, *The Sailor's Word Book: An illustrated digest of nautical terms* (London: Blackie & Son, 1867), Project Guttenberg EBook, 2008. https://archive.org/stream/thesailorswordbo26000gut/26000-0.txt
24. Hellyer, *Voyage to Van Diemen's Land*, 16.
25. Ibid., 25.
26. Mary Leman Grimstone, *Scrapbook*, 49b.
27. Ibid.
28. Ibid.
29. Hellyer, *Voyage to Van Diemen's Land*, 25.
30. Ibid.
31. Ibid.
32. Ibid., 26.
33. Ibid., 26.
34. Colonial Secretary's Correspondence, indexed under Adey, Stephen & Wogan, Mary, affidavit by James Rowley, TAHO, CSO1/1/29 (510).
35. Hellyer, *Voyage to Van Diemen's Land*, 31.
36. Mary Leman Grimstone, *Scrapbook*, 49a.
37. *Hobart Town Gazette*, March 11, 1826, 2.
38. *Hobart Town Gazette*, Police Office, Saturday, March 18, 1826, 2.

39. Ibid.
40. *Hobart Town Gazette*, Supreme Court, Saturday, April 1, 1826, 2.
41. Ibid.
42. *Hobart Town Gazette*, March 18, 1826, 2.
43. Ibid.
44. Supreme Court Minutes, March 23–25, 1826, TAHO, SC32/1/1. https://stors.tas.gov.au/SC32-1-1$init=SC32-1-1p146jpg
45. *Hobart Town Gazette*, April 1, 1826, 2.
46. Ibid.
47. Colonial Secretary's Correspondence, TAHO, CSO1/1/29 (510).
48. Van Diemen's Land Company Court of Directors to Edward Curr, August 30, 1826, Inward Despatch No. 20. TAHO VDL193/1/1.
49. *Colonial Times and Tasmanian Advertiser*, Ship News, Friday, April 28, 1826, 2.
50. *Hobart Town Gazette*, Freight and Passage, Saturday, April 29, 1826, 1.
51. Mark Howard, "Masters of the Sydney Whaling Fleet, 1805–1896," Descent, Vol. 44, No. 2 (June 2014): 73–96.
52. Hellyer, *Voyage to Van Diemen's Land*, 5.
53. Hellyer, *Voyage to Van Diemen's Land*, 11.
54. Mary Leman Grimstone, Scrapbook, 49c.

James Scott: surveyor, explorer and pioneer of North-East Tasmania

JOHN BESWICK

Few Tasmanian settlers have achieved the distinction of having a town or district of their adopted state named after them. Whilst some geographical features were named for individuals, the dominant trend in the colonial era was to name places after a town or village in the "Old Country".

One whose standing was such as to justify defiance of that trend was surveyor James Scott, a native of the Scottish borderlands, who became renowned as a superb bushman and redoubtable explorer, a man of exceptional physical stamina and mental energy. A kinsman of Sir Walter Scott, the famous Scottish author, James was born in the Parish of Legerwood in Berwickshire, on March 10, 1810, the sixth child of tenant farmer George Scott and his wife Betty Pringle.[1] He was employed as a clerk in the office of Sir Walter Scott at Melrose Abbey before migrating to Van Diemen's Land at the age of 22.[2]

James had been preceded in his migration to the colony by his eldest brother Thomas, ten years his senior, who arrived in 1820, and a second brother, George, who came two years later. Thomas had been trained as a surveyor in Scotland and, after a short period of employment as Superintendent of Government Stock, was appointed Assistant Surveyor under G. W. Evans, the recently promoted Deputy Surveyor-General. Thomas was very active in surveying and exploration during the following years and composed a map of Van Diemen's Land, published in 1824,[3] which incorporated more detail of land

James Scott (1810–1884).
Sourced from descendants of James Scott, courtesy of J. Jennings

grants than any other up to that time. He took up several property holdings, including the extensive Mt Morriston Estate, near Ross, and Cocked Hat Hill Estate at Breadalbane, which was subdivided. His brother George managed Mt Morriston for many years, developing it as a superfine wool property.

After James arrived in 1832, Thomas taught him the profession of surveying, the younger brother obviously proving an apt pupil. In 1836, Thomas took two years leave to return to Scotland and recommended that James be appointed as his *locum tenens*, with the salary to be shared between them. When Thomas applied for an extension of his leave from 1838, his request was refused and he subsequently resigned.[4]

James was appointed by Lt.-Governor Sir John Franklin to fill the vacancy created by Thomas' resignation. However, just a year later, the government changed its practice of employing staff surveyors and introduced a system of engaging qualified surveyors on contract as required. Under the new system, James was named in a list of 12 individuals advertised in the press, who "received the sanction of the government to act as contract surveyors".[5] He wrote to Thomas that he was happy with this arrangement, as it left him free to do private work, at which he was more efficient than most other surveyors. He had taken up residence in Thomas' house "Bowhill" at Glen Dhu in Launceston, and for much of the next 20 years or so he was the only surveyor permanently based in the northern region. According to later reports, he became the pre-eminent authority on real estate properties in the north.[6]

Aside from his surveying work, much of James' time during this period was taken up with looking after the business affairs of Thomas, who remained in Scotland for the rest of his life, and writing detailed letters to his brother reporting on those affairs. These included many property dealings, both on behalf of Thomas and on his own behalf. At the time of Thomas' death in 1855, James estimated the value of his brother's estate at £107,800.[7]

On October 14, 1845, James married Agnes Mathie McGown, eldest daughter of David McGown of Distillery Creek, a former distiller from Sterling, Scotland. He commented in a letter to Thomas that, "they are very respectable quiet and frugal people – and I think I have made a very good marriage". The couple would eventually have 11 children.

■

Undoubtedly, the field of endeavour for which James Scott is best remembered is his work in the exploration and opening up of the inland parts of the north-east, which remained largely unexplored until the 1850s. Prior to this, while employed by the government in April-May 1836, he was commissioned to undertake a survey of the coastline between Pipers River and the mouth of the Ringarooma River. Over a period of seven weeks, supported by three men and a dray drawn by a team of six bullocks to carry their tents and equipment, he surveyed along the coast and up some of the larger streams for a short distance, crossing rivers and meeting up with a few isolated settlers. Probably the most notable of these was Captain Charles Hardwicke, who was first to take a grazing lease in the Waterhouse area. At the Ringarooma River, Scott saw an overseer employed by the Rev. Dr W. H. Browne on a grant of land he held there and met up with another surveyor named Dawson, apparently by prior arrangement.[8]

On the way back, James and his party happened to meet three sealers and two aborigines in the vicinity of Weymouth. One of the sealers was James

Munro from Preservation Island, who lived on the island from 1819 until his death in 1845 and became known as the "King of the Eastern Straitsmen".

In later years Scott was employed by the government to further survey some of the rivers and streams on the north coast, including an expedition of several kilometres up the Great Forester River. In March 1840, he reported having been "around the North-East and East coasts with Captain Boyd", then Deputy Surveyor-General, and another surveyor, Thomas Lewis, who had earlier carried out surveys on the coast. They started from George Town, travelling on horseback, passing Ringarooma (river mouth), Cape Portland and St George's River, returning by St Patrick's Head and the Break O' Day Plains, being "out for 10 days". James noted that he had not seen any good land worth taking![9]

His first major foray into the inland north-East came in 1852, when he was asked by the government to investigate the feasibility of a direct overland bridle road between Launceston and Cape Portland. In response to this request, he wrote to the Deputy Surveyor-General on March 22 proposing to take a line from J. Anderson's location at St Patricks River, on a north-easterly course, passing over high land where the rivers would be small enough to obviate the need for expensive bridge construction, and thence to the south-east of Mt Cameron towards Cape Portland. He said he could not estimate how long the journey would take, owing to the probability of thick scrub being encountered.[10] Ten days later he was instructed to proceed with this proposal.

Remarkably, by April 19 he was reporting back after completing the assignment in just 11 days, having covered a total distance of at least 180 kilometres on foot. His report tells how the chosen route took him past Mt Maurice, which he named, and into the upper valley of the Ringarooma River, which he mistook for the Great Forester.

His report continues, "The line passes over a low and rich soil covered with dense scrubs, and half a mile of excellent dry land with small timber covered with nettles etc., but easily cleared; beyond that river the land continues good for one mile when it crosses another large stream – and ascends the tier dividing the (tributaries of the Ringarooma River). This tier is covered with almost impenetrable scrubs to the summit of a low part where I passed it. The country was level until I reached the dividing range between the first and second branches of the Ringarooma, on this tier the rocks on the top rise, in huge boulders and appear next to impossible for stock without a great outlay – it was with great difficulty a man can scramble up on hands and knees between the rocks ... also the ridge beyond the second branch appeared more steep and difficult, which induced me to follow down the second branch (probably the Cascade River) to the junction with the main river, in hopes of finding a more easy passage – but the tiers appeared to extend unbroken all the distance and ended abruptly at the river, so steep and rocky that no horse could pass them. The tiers still continued very high and rocky until coming to the fifth branch, when the country falls gradually, becomes free of scrubs with stringy bark forests … I marked the trees well to the second branch of the Ringarooma, after which I followed in sight the course of the river generally – and made the open country between the Ringarooma and Mussel Roe Rivers, at the head of "Harden's Ravine" (near Gladstone), on the evening of Sunday the 11th in the midst of heavy rain. In consequence of the dense scrubs and heavy rains I did not return the same way – but took the open country along the coast and arrived here on Friday evening the 16th."[11]

Unsurprisingly, Scott concluded that the idea of a bridle road to Cape Portland along the route he had taken was not feasible, due to the rugged terrain and lack of good feed for stock, and recommended instead a route closer to the north coast via Pipers River. However, he had discovered something else that really excited him. The rich red basaltic soil of the area around the upper reaches of the Ringarooma River and its tributaries drew him back to the locality several times during the next two years. Within the same year (1852), he returned to mark out a block of 640 acres that he applied to take up, together with an adjoining block in the name of his brother George.[12]

In September he wrote, in a letter to Thomas, that he was "going off for three weeks to mark a road from here (Launceston) to Cape Portland by way of Pipers River, which the Government intends to open up"[13] (his recommended route). But in spite of having declared the inland route of his first trek impractical, just nine months after that journey he wrote to the Colonial Secretary on behalf of "owners and lessees of land situated at the Great Forester River", advising that they had engaged him to open up a line of communication from Launceston to that locality and requesting a grant of 40 pounds towards the project.[14] He had apparently decided that the richness of the soil warranted the development of a road to that point and had encouraged others to join him in applying for land there. The Colonial Office agreed to the request for a grant, subject to a sketch of the line, and on November 4, 1853, Scott reported having completed the road as far as Lot 441, purchased by Captain J. H. Kay.[15]

In April 1854 he wrote, again to Thomas, "I have taken a lot of the best soil in the island – it is 40 miles from here on the Ringarooma River and 25 miles from the sea – with 2 fine streams of water through it and the river in front ... George has taken another lot behind in his name but I mean to pay for it and get both lots so as to have a good farm ..."[16] Contemporary Lands department charts[17] confirm several lots fronting onto the Ringarooma River, as surveyed by James Scott himself in January and February 1854, and show the road he marked from Launceston to the Ringarooma River, roughly following his original route past Mt Maurice and following the Maurice River down into the Ringarooma Valley. It would be another 10 years before he began seriously developing his property, citing as his reason the high cost of labour caused by the Victorian gold rush.

The question now arises as to how the Scottsdale district, through which Scott did not pass on his journeys to and from the upper Ringarooma, came to be known as "Scott's New Country", a precursor to the later naming of Scottsdale by popular demand. A possible explanation may lie in an account of an exploratory expedition, supposed to have occurred in 1855 and described by Thomas Hogarth, another pioneer who knew Scott personally, which was first published in the *Cyclopedia of Tasmania*.[18] Hogarth, claiming corroboration by Mr Richard Saggers, who had accompanied Scott to the Ringarooma "on his second trip", describes a journey similar in some respects to Scott's first expedition. This account describes an apparently different route, beginning near the headwaters of the North Esk River in the vicinity of Roses Tier and taking a beeline from there to the north coast near Waterhouse Sheep Station. The return journey, as recounted by Hogarth, was again different, after heading westwards along the coastal plain for 12 to 15 miles, turning south on a line parallel to the first and emerging from the unknown country at "Didlem" (Diddleum Plains), north-east of Mt Barrow. The writer asserts that on his outward journey, "Mr Scott tracked right through the fertile lands of the Ringarooma, camping for the night on the spot where now stands the Legerwood homestead; on the return journey, from the coast to Didlem, he ran right through the fertile lands of Scottsdale."

This account was long believed to be a description of Scott's first journey, but it was proved not to be so when Scott's own report of his 1852 expedition was discovered. Unfortunately, no official report of the 1855 journey has survived; however if there was indeed such an expedition, in which Scott discovered the fertile land of the Scottsdale district, it could explain why there was no taking up of land there until after 1855. And it could also account for the immediate locality of Scottsdale being shown on an 1859 Lands Department chart as "Scott's New Country".[19] The chart shows a number of blocks that had been surveyed in late 1858, including one located to James Scott.

Scott's "Legerwood" homestead, 1881.
Sourced from descendants of James Scott, courtesy of J. Jennings

The same chart shows a "Line of Road (from Myrtle Bank) to the Ringarooma" at Branxholm, marked by J. R. Scott and D. Stronach in March 1859. J. R. (James Reid) Scott was James' nephew, whom he had persuaded to take up the "Branxholm Estate", down river from his own selections. (Branxholme is the name of a hamlet in the Scottish Borders, which is the setting of Sir Walter Scott's novel, *The Lay of the Last Minstrel*.) The above chart also shows a "Springfield Town Reserve" to the south of the Scottsdale district, as "Proposed by Mr Scott in May 1859", suggesting again that James himself was indeed active in the area at that time. A town reserve created around this time at Scott's New Country was inexplicably named Ellesmere, the name of a town in Shropshire, England.

James named his property on the Ringarooma "Legerwood", after his birthplace in Scotland. According to Hogarth, who claimed to have felled the first tree to be felled for clearing purposes at Legerwood, this occurred in 1864 together with the construction of a cottage and enclosure of a garden. The Assessment Roll for 1866 shows James Scott as controlling 2180 acres of bush at Ringarooma River, having presumably taken over some lots relinquished by original selectors. James Reid Scott is shown as owning 820 acres (at Branxholm) but is believed to have controlled much more. He did not, however, reside there for very long, as he married, was elected to Parliament and lived in Hobart, sadly dying at the age of 38 after having nine children.[20]

From about 1860, James had scaled back his surveying operations and progressively devoted more of his time to community service. A stalwart of Chalmers Presbyterian Church, he was twice elected as an Alderman of the City of Launceston, served as a director of several companies, and for a term as Chairman of the Launceston General Hospital Board. Appointed as a Justice of the Peace in 1862, he sat on the bench for local court hearings on numerous occasions. He was elected as a Member of the House of Assembly in the Tasmanian Parliament, for George Town from 1869 to 1877 and for South Launceston from 1878 until his death on October 15, 1884,[21] always remaining independent of party affiliations.

He died of liver disease aged 74 at his home, Bowhill, "in perfect enjoyment of all his faculties", described in an obituary[22] as having "secured for himself, through his sterling honesty and independence of character, the respect and esteem of all with whom he came in contact". It was said that his "tenacity of memory" was such that he could give an accurate description of any country or district he had once surveyed.

Nine years later, in March 1893, lobbying by the local community culminated in a unanimous petition from the Ellesmere (Scottsdale) Town Board and a gazetted proclamation under the Town Boards Act of 1891 changing the name of the town of Ellesmere to that of Scottsdale, in memory of the esteemed surveyor.[23] Scott's Legerwood property was bequeathed to two of his sons, George and Thomas,[24] and later divided into several farms for sale. Another son, Robert, purchased and took up residence at the property named "Woodlands".[25] Some of his descendants remain in the area today.

■ ■ ■

ENDNOTES

1. National Records of Scotland, (Old Parish Births 749/ 10 185 Legerwood), p. 185 of 203.
2. Crawford, G. H., "The Scotts: Thomas, George and James" (A paper read to the Tasmanian Historical Association in October 1964), 4–6.

3. Libraries Tasmania, Chart of Van Diemen's Land, Thomas Scott (AUTAS 139593842).
4. G. H. Crawford, "The Scotts", 7.
5. *Hobart Town Courier*, February 22, 1839, 2.
6. *Launceston Examiner*, October 16, 1884, 2.
7. D. J. L. Archer, *The Scott Letters: VDL & Scotland* (Launceston, Tas., Regal Publications), 6.
8. J. Jennings, *A History of Bridport* (Bridport, Tas., J & B. Jennings, 1983), 7–11.
9. Archer, *The Scott Letters*, 85.
10. E. Hookway, J. Jennings and P. Page, *Scott's New Country* (Scottsdale, Tas., Scott's New Country Committee) 10.
11. Hookway, Jennings and Page, *Scott's New Country*, 10–12.
12. A memorandum signed by the Collector of Internal Revenue, dated June 22, 1853, confirms amongst other purchases, that James Scott had completed the purchase of Lot 279, 640 acres, at Great Forester River. Archives of Tasmania LSD1/1/76 p. 609.
13. Archer, *The Scott Letters*, 361.
14. Crawford, "The Scotts", 10.
15. Crawford, "The Scotts", 11.
16. Crawford, "The Scotts", 12.
17. Libraries Tasmania, AF396-1-497 and 506.
18. *Cyclopedia of Tasmania, An Historical and Commercial Review*, Vol. II, (Hobart 1899–1900, Maitland and Krone), 324–325.
19. Libraries Tasmania, AF398-1-144.
20. Crawford, "The Scotts", 19.
21. S. Bennett and B. Bennett, *Biographical Register of the Tasmanian Parliament 1851–1960* (Canberra, Australian National University Press).
22. *Launceston Examiner*, October 16, 1884, 2.
23. Hookway, Jennings and Page, *Scott's New Country*, 80–82.
24. Archer, *The Scott Letters*, 9.
25. Letter from Mrs Jean Walsh of "Woodlands" Legerwood, a daughter of Robert Scott (January 1987).

The Goldie incident revisited

The Tasmanians ... were [largely] swept out of existence in a war of extermination waged by European immigrants.

H. G. Wells, *The War of the Worlds*[1]

DAVID FABER

COOEE, VAN DIEMEN'S LAND, AUGUST 21, 1829

Today, the Burnie Regional Museum commemorates the establishment in 1828 of the port-city by the Van Diemen's Land Company, the last British chartered joint stock land company. As a teenager during the Whitlam years, attending Burnie High School under the adoptive surname of Clements and passionate about history, I never heard from a single teacher of the pioneering company. The pedagogical principle of an early focus on local affairs in teaching history appears to have been overlooked in my day. History seemed to have happened elsewhere, perhaps in our Gallipoli Iliad, in which, I had known from infancy, a few locals had participated. But epic feet have trodden our home soil too, for example during the invasion and conquest of Van Diemen's Land.

This oversight is surprising, as the history of the Tasmanian north-west is arrestingly interesting. The VDL Company was as armed in its way as the East India Company. It conquered the north-west by ambushes, dealing out death through its servants to the indigenous inhabitants, shattering their nations in the space of a few years. European settlement on the coast began more darkly and dramatically than many imagine, even to this day.

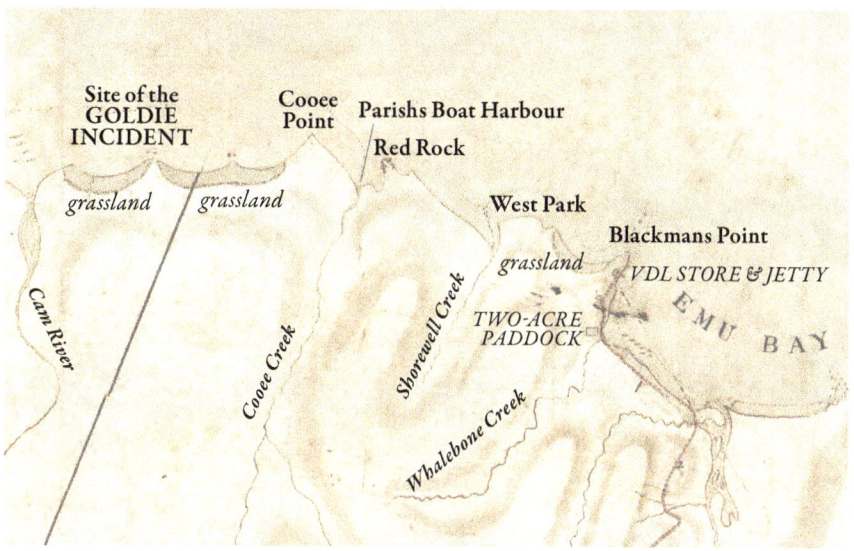

Map showing the location of the Goldie incident.
Portion of Henry Hellyer's 1832 map superimposed with information supplied by Brian Rollins.

This can be seen in the details of the "important" event, known to Tasmanian historians as "the Goldie incident".[2] The general public, however, has yet to be fully seized of it. It regards an unprovoked murder (recognised as such even by Keith Windschuttle, although he downplays its significance)[3] during a "gin raid",[4] an illegal attempt at abduction of non-combatant women by VDL Co servants under the effectively para-military command of its Agricultural Superintendent, Alexander Goldie. It occurred while the island was under racially targeted martial law, declared by Lieutenant Governor Arthur in November 1828,[5] on Cooee Beach, west of the present-day site of Burnie High School.[6] It ought to be common knowledge for every inhabitant of the coast, not to say the state and the nation.

The more we understand the past, the better we understand ourselves, and that increases control over our own destiny. This is especially the case in the coast's contemporary post-industrial era, when historically informed cultural tourism will play an increasingly important role. And the importance of the matter to reconciliation on the coast goes without saying.

The Goldie incident is best described in Goldie's own well-spun words. On September 16, 1829, nearly four weeks after the incident, Goldie reported particulars to his superior, Company Chief Agent Edward Curr Senior. He

Cooee Beach looking to the site of the Goldie incident.
Photograph by Brian Rollins

carefully threw the responsibility for the killing on the party of convict servants under his authority:

> The day the *Fanny* last sailed from this (21 August) I was putting up a shed for rams at [in fact towards] the Cam, and when looking at the feed, I came upon a mob of Natives. Seeing them on the Point [at Cooee] I returned to the men and determined to endeavour to take some of them. For this purpose, I took my horse and the men, one gun and a couple of axes. On getting within 200 yards of them we were observed and they began to make off. I ordered the men to keep outside while I took the scrub. This had the desired effect and the natives kept along the sands. Russell fired at one just as she was taking the scrub and shot her. She was very badly hit about the bottom and belly, and she must have died. I rode down another woman in the scrub and before I returned with her the men had killed the other. The woman that was shot had a child about 6 years old (a girl) which we also got. I saw another three, but whether there were any more, or any men among them I cannot say …[7]

Van Diemen's Land Company's establishment at Emu Bay from the east. Drawing by VDL Co. employee John Hicks Hutchinson.
Dr J. H. Hutchinson, Emu Bay, 1830, VDL 261/700, TAHO

The rest of the letter confidentially detailed how the other Aboriginal woman had been illegally enslaved in the company's service and put to work experimentally, a point relevant to the company economically and to the colonial administration politically.[8] Subsequently, the character clash between Goldie and Curr came to a head over the incident and the Cape Grim Massacre, with Curr provokingly accusing Goldie of having aggressively exceeded established company policy and practice near the Emu Bay settlement in committing "so flagrant a prima facie case of murder".[9] Goldie was dismayed, for Curr was the director of the lethal, not to say barbarous, "native" policy of the company in the north-west.[10] It was also dangerous language, given that Curr had been charged by Arthur with investigating the matter.[11] Goldie retaliated by undermining Curr with the company's servants. He advised these employees that they would be exposed to capital criminal prosecution for implementing company policy towards Aboriginal people in practice.[12] This was effectively legislated with extreme prejudice on the ground by Curr as company Chief Agent, in violation of the paternalistic, civilising, assimilationist intent of the London directors, conscience-stricken at the forbearance due to the indigenous landowners for their expropriation, preferably by "civilising" and exploiting them as labourers.[13] Curr showed much more alacrity in safeguarding his authority than in investigating as Resident Magistrate the Cooee killing, dragging his heels for months. This he did only at the behest of Arthur, whom Goldie had dragged into the dispute by informing His Excellency of the company policy on which he (Goldie) had consistently acted.[14]

In struggling with each other, both men appear as duplicitous as they could be brutal,[15] arguably typically of the managerial gentlefolk of the day, contemptuous of their racial and class "inferiors".[16] If so, this class-driven behaviour would tend to bear out the 1977 thesis of Bronwyn Dessailly, criticised by Geoff Lennox in 1990, that Curr was in reality an exponent of the colonial "exterminationist" party, although it may reasonably be doubted if this evasive, diffident and calculating man was openly so.[17] These observations correspond also with the class and ethnic nature of British imperialism in the era 1688–1914 as analysed by Cain & Hopkin in their seminal magnum opus on British imperialism, which Windschuttle attempts to recruit to argue that genocide and ethnic cleansing did not occur in Van Diemen's Land, because the British as opposed to the notorious Spanish practiced a kinder, gentler form of conquest, informed by humanitarian imperialist values and practices.[18]

This is a tendentious misinterpretation of Cain & Hopkin's thesis of the "gentlemanly capitalism" of British global expansionism. This indeed got underway as a private, civil society, aristocratically managed and financed project in England's first colony, Ireland, in 1170, by the infamous "Strongbow", Richard de Clare, during the reign but in advance of the royal endorsement of Henry II, which came later in that decade with his confirmation as Earl of Pembroke.[19] Given the Irish experience of English rule, it can readily be seen that the record of English expansionism was hardly benign, howsoever rapacious were other imperialists. The innovative capitalist role of the English aristocracy and gentry from the 17th century on cannot be doubted, as exemplified by such enterprising lords as the modernising Whig revolutionary Anthony Ashley Cooper, 1st Earl of Shaftesbury,[20] (the patron of the proto-liberal ideologue John Locke, an advocate for both slavery and colonisation). English imperialism never baulked at genocide and ethnic cleansing or discrimination on racial and class grounds in the cause of empire. Even those who fought the slave trade and afterwards asserted the human rights of indigenous peoples tended not to question imperialism as such, which involved these historical abuses. After all, Liberal Imperialism was a feature of Westminster politics right into the late 19th and early 20th centuries. Indeed, one superannuated exponent, Sir Ronald

Munro-Ferguson [later Viscount Novar] served as the proconsular supervisor of the Australian Great War effort.

That said, it was not strange that colonial Solicitor General Alfred Stephen determined, in respect of the Goldie incident, against a prosecution on the convenient technicality that the woman had been fatally shot under martial law as an enemy rather than slain as a prisoner with an axe.[21] This had been done as a coup de grace by a 17-year-old company servant in the squad of shepherds, Richard Sweetling.[22] The Colonial Office was relieved that Arthur had abstained from intervening in what it saw as a dispute between company officers.[23] The colonial press meanwhile resented the company's privileged access to land, and Curr was known as "the Potentate of the North",[24] because of his dual commercial and legal authority.[25]

Death was thus dealt out to an Aboriginal woman, probably of the Table Cape-based Tommeginer nation, in Curr's state within a colony within an empire. The manner in which the matter was swept under the carpet was perfectly in keeping with Curr's stated view that Aboriginal "aggression" obliged the government to authorise a war of extermination to guarantee clear land title to settlers, devoid of obligations to prior inhabitants,[26] a policy of genocide which Curr implemented and sustained on company land until his services were terminated due to his irascible clashes with the colonial government in 1842.[27]

The politics of dispossession has evolved over time, from notions of colonial right to concepts of historical responsibility.[28] For example, in 1937, a prominent British imperialist gave evidence to the Peel Commission, which was investigating the morass that the 1917 Balfour Declaration had created in Palestine. He ventured the opinion that:

> I do not agree that the dog in the manger has the final right to the manger, even though he may have lain there for a very long time. I do not admit that right. I do not admit, for instance, that a great wrong has been done to the red Indians of America, or the black people of Australia. I do not admit that a wrong has been done to those people by the fact that a stronger race, a higher-grade race, a more worldly-wise race, to put it that way, has come in and taken their place.[29]

In his day Winston Churchill was the voice of conventional opinion. Few would be so blatantly racist as to dare to be so frank now. The Goldie incident was in fact a criminal act of abduction and murder, carried out by bonded servants of a capitalist firm, acting under the instructions of a gentleman official of the company. It was implementing in its own commercial interest a policy of de facto dispossession, shrouded in a rhetoric of reluctant displacement and civilising intent. The British Empire and its colonial administration wilfully looked the other way. Forgoing the colonial enterprise which entailed ethnic cleansing in north-west Van Diemen's Land was never contemplated. The invasion, conquest and settlement of the Coast arose in a global context during the 19th century heyday of British imperial capitalism. A Royal Charter, £1,000,000 of London capital, three parliamentary members and an Act of the Westminster Parliament were involved.

In the 20th century, local historians tended to apologise for the Curr's conduct during the pioneering of the region, a tendency corrected by 21st century scholarship.[30] The company of course continues to operate in the region. It would be churlish to suggest that its present Chinese owners are responsible for the crimes of Goldie and Curr. Indeed, if only out of enlightened self-interest in tourist revenue from its property, the VDL Co exercises good corporate citizenship. These considerations dictate facilitation of community awareness and historical understanding. The company now positively engages with the Aboriginal community, employing indigenous workers who, amongst other employments, guide tourists. It is possible to tour, for example, the massacre site at Cape Grim, its reality attested after much controversy by colonial documents, indigenous oral tradition and historical investigation.[31] Some may feel that it would be better to avert our eyes from such things. But reality is a sounder, firmer foundation for self-understanding than romanticised notions of the pioneering spirit and its latter-day work ethic legacy. Recognising the trauma inflicted on the Coast's indigenous population during VDL Co settlement is an important step towards settling our fundamental account with the historical past and achieving a measure of social justice and maturity. At Wynyard the main street is named after Goldie as a pioneer, despite the criminal acts he commissioned, of which the bulk of the townsfolk remain unaware; unaware indeed that the traditional name of the street refers to him at all.

Historical enquiry enfranchises the future through engaging with the reality of the past. In that sense, history is an ongoing discursive debate, and the history wars are always with us, more or less, as interest wrestles culturally with interest, hopefully without the unscrupulous, white-blindfold, denialist rhetoric of certain commentators of the *Quadrant* stable. Having a principled ethical and critical, logical point of view is no impediment to historical objectivity. On the contrary, it is necessary to historical evaluation. As Oxford historiographer Robin George Collingwood rightly stated, in that ongoing discussion, we aim, not at finality but at an ever-increasing depth of objective insight, both ethical and pragmatic.[32]

■ ■ ■

ENDNOTES

1. *H. G. Wells: The science fiction*, Vol. I, (London: Phoenix Giants, 1995), 186.
2. The designation of the so-called "Goldie incident" has been confirmed by Murray Johnson & Ian McFarlane, *Van Diemen's Land: An Aboriginal history* (Sydney: University of New South Wales Press, 2015), 184. See also their evaluation of its importance.
3. Keith Windschuttle, *The Fabrication of Aboriginal History*, Vol. I, Van Diemen's Land 1803–47, (Sydney: McLeay Press, 2002), 256; I concur with the critical assessment of his notice in Ian McFarlane, "Cape Grim", in Robert Manne, ed., *Whitewash: On Keith Windschuttle's fabrication of Aboriginal history*, (Melbourne: Black Inc. Agenda, 2003), 283.
4. Nicholas Clements, *The Black War* (St Lucia: University of Queensland Press, 2015), 68–71.
5. Nick Brodie, *The Vandemonian War* (Melbourne: Hardie Grant, 2017), 28–9.
6. The site is designated by Johnson & McFarlane, cit., 183 & 185.
7. Cited by Geoff Lennox, "The Van Diemen's Land Company & the Tasmanian Aborigines: A reappraisal", in *Tasmanian Historical Research Association: Papers & Proceedings*, Vol. 37, No. 4, December 1990, 180.
8. Cited in Johnson & McFarlane, cit., 184–5, & McFarlane cit., 284. On the company practice of abduction and enslavement and the Company's London Directors' policy of humanitarian imperialism through civilising introduction to work of Aboriginals as labour, see their despatch of 11 June 18 1828, cited in Lennox, cit., 167.
9. Edward Curr, "Highfield", Circular Head, to Alexander Goldie, October 8, 1829.
10. McFarlane, "Cape Grim", cit., 290. For evidence of Curr's barbarous tendencies, see his pursuit of an Aboriginal party at Burghley in the hope of decapitating a quarry with a view to displaying the head as a deterrent against incursions, in Johnson & McFarlane, cit., 186.
11. McFarlane, cit., 283.
12. Johnson & McFarlane, cit., 186.
13. Lennox, cit., 167.
14. Johnson & McFarlane, cit., 185 & McFarlane cit., 283.

15. McFarlane, cit., 296.
16. Ibid., 296.
17. Lennox, cit., 166. In contradiction of Lennox and Windschuttle, see McFarlane, cit., 290–2.
18. Windschuttle, cit., 30f.
19. *The History Today Who's Who of British History*, 179.
20. Ibid., 202–3.
21. On Stephen's role in the case, see Johnson & McFarlane cit., 187–8.
22. Sweetling is identified by Johnson & McFarlane, cit., 184 &186; his tender age is noted by Windschuttle, cit., 256. The axe, one of two issued by Goldie as weapons with the musket handed out for the pursuit of the Aboriginal party, severed the jugular vein in what would have been a very bloody despatch. Sweetling's youth makes plausible his statement to the Company's Emu Bay storekeeper that he was "so agitated at the time [of executing the coup de grace, that] he did not know what he was doing and that if he had had time to reflect he did not think he could have done it". See Statement of Thomas Watson, Storekeeper for the Van Diemen's Land Company, December 17, 1829, [to Edward Curr, Company Chief Agent & Justice of the Peace for Van Diemen's Land & Dependencies], Appendix 9 in Ian McFarlane, *Beyond Awakening – The Aboriginal Tribes of North West Tasmania: A History*, (Hobart: Fullers Bookshop, Riawunna & Community, Place & Heritage Research Unit, University of Tasmania, 2008), 235.
23. Colonial Under-Secretary Lord Howick's note approving the colonial administration's diffident handling of the case is reported by A. G. L. Shaw at note 22 in his unpaginated Introduction to *Van Diemen's Land: Copies of all correspondence between Lt-Governor Arthur & … the Secretary … for the Colonies … [re] the military operations … carried on against the Aboriginal inhabitants …* (Hobart: Tasmanian Historical Research Association, 1971).
24. John West, *The History of Tasmania*, (London: Angus & Robertson, 1971), 274.
25. A. L. Meston, *The Van Diemen's Land Company 1825–1842* (Launceston: Museum Committee, City Council, 1958), 42–5.
26. McFarlane, cit., 290. For Curr's class consciousness and overarching colonialism, see his *An Account of the Colony of Van Diemen's Land*, designed primarily for the use of emigrants, (London: George Cowie, 1824).
27. Manne, in "Conclusion", *Whitewash*, cit., 383–4 on his policy and practice of ethnic cleansing, and the note by K. M. Dallas in Meston, cit., 50.
28. For an international review citing the Australian case of issues re national historical responsibility for crimes against humanity, see Elazar Barkan, *The Guilt of Nations: Restitution & negotiating historical injustices*, (New York: Norton & Co., 2000)
29. Cited, Bernard Regan, *The Balfour Declaration: Empire, the Mandate & Resistance in Palestine* (London: Verso, 2017), 202.
30. Lennox's diffident distinctions in criticising Dessailly for having in a supposedly "simplistic" way made too much of the reservations of contemporaries and the historian Brian Plomley are excessive; nevertheless, even Lennox assesses Meston as too apologetic regarding the "native" policy of Curr and the Company. See Lennox, cit., 166.
31. McFarlane, cit., 227–98

32. "The Nature & Aims of a Philosophy of History" in William Debbins, ed., *Collingwood: Essays in the Philosophy of History*, (Austin: University of Texas Press 1968), 53–4, & William H. Dray & W. J. van der Dussen, eds., *Collingwood: The principles of history & other writings in the philosophy of history*, (New York: Oxford University Press, 1999), 158.

Embodied charity in the Maternal and Dorcas Society

MADONNA GREHAN

Snapshot Hobart Town, the mid-1830s: it's a bustling metropolis with a population of roughly 14,000 of the new white-settler variety, free and convict.[1] Writing of his impressions of the place, George Best, an English immigrant, was captivated by its beautiful harbour, multiple warehouses and homes visible from the River Derwent as the ship approached Sullivan's Cove and the wharf. Set against the towering Mount Wellington, the welcoming vista conveyed a sense of order and optimism. There were green sloping lawns, meandering streets leading up a gentle northerly incline, and pretty gardens. On the surface, Hobart Town offered nothing but a comfortable outlook for those seeking better prospects.

Having escaped from the confines of ships, the most pressing issue for newcomers was finding somewhere to live, with plenty of competition from fellow passengers. Hobart Town's housing market had relaxed somewhat by 1836, as established colonists relinquished properties for more salubrious environs in the surrounding countryside. *Bent's News* reported that weatherboard houses in Hobart Town fetched £60 per annum in rent.[2] Murray Street, leading directly from the wharf, already had 94 houses.[3]

Once an immigrant's accommodation was settled, next was the excitement of retrieving belongings from the ship, packed in England months ago, the foundations for a new life. Some people were well-prepared, courtesy of immigrant guides which opined on the weather, when to sow which crop, the colonial administration, schools, religion and other important matters. Guides and almanacks advised on the economy of arriving equipped,[4] but there were no guarantees that precious goods would survive the long and arduous journey by sea. Poorly secured furniture splintered in rough weather and was gnawed at by hungry rats in the dank holds of ships. Moths and other creatures were aided in their destruction by inundations of salt water and humidity-generated mould. These conditions obliterated carpets, bedding, clothing and valued belongings.

It was possible to buy locally, should goods arrive spoiled. Woolley's Upholstery Warehouse in Hobart Town supplied Brussels and Kidderminster carpets, hearth rugs and druggels.[5] H. Solomon's, at Victoria House in Elizabeth Street, carried an astonishing range from cutlery to purse mounts, tassels, shirt studs, jewellery, hair lockets, flat tableware and head bandeaus.[6] At J. Wait's, 50 Murray Street, women could find "decidedly [a] most choice collection of ladies' Dunstable and fancy Tuscan bonnets, surpassing any ever yet imported" as well as gingham, and muslins with Peruvian, Mexican and oriental patterns.[7]

But, in this far-off metropolis, goods from halfway around the world that had arrived safely came at a price.

Thus, for at least some immigrants, a good start in Van Diemen's Land was contingent to a degree on good luck. And despite the best-laid plans, people's hopes and dreams of a new and propitious life could vanish in an instant, or in a slow spiral of debt, if work was not immediately available for the family breadwinner. If husbands, gainfully employed, became ill and unable to work, women who had emigrated without extended family or friends were particularly vulnerable. Newspapers called on the government to pitch in, complaining that free settlers down on their luck had less support than convicts.[8] But without social security nets, the wretchedness of poverty could be inescapable.

The plight of women and their children thrust into the dire realm of poverty was recognised by a network of 22 philanthropically-minded women in 1835. They established the Maternal and Dorcas Society (Dorcas Society) which proved to be one of Tasmania's most enduring charitable services.[9] To convey the legitimacy of this embryonic organisation, the founding committee secured a prominent woman as patron in Mrs Arthur, wife of the Governor.

Hobart's Dorcas Society was founded primarily to "assist destitute married women during the time of their confinement" and secondly to extend

> *Hobart Town Maternal & Dorcas Society.*
> Patroness—Mrs. ARTHUR.
>
> THE attention of many Ladies in Hobart town having been lately given to the formation of some fixed plan for the relief of *poor married women*, during the time of their confinement, combining the general assistance of other *destitute poor*,—the attendance of any ladies who may be inclined to co-operate in this benevolent design, is requested on Monday next the 17th August, at 2 o'clock, at the house of Mrs. HOWE, in Elizabeth-street.

> MATERNAL AND DORCAS SOCIETY.—Some of the Ladies of Hobart Town, actuated by the true spirit of philanthropy, which is so characteristic of the British Fair, have established, under the above designation, a society for the purpose of affording temporary relief and assistance to poor women during their confinement. Such a society reflects the highest credit on its founders, and if there be any Lady who has not yet enrolled her name as a member, we trust she will lose no time in doing so at once. At the present time there is a wide field for benevolence. Poverty and gaunt misery walk abroad in their most horrid forms; and, therefore, the charity of the wealthy is now more than ever required.

Newspaper reports of the foundation of the
Hobart Town Maternal and Dorcas Society in 1835.

relief to the poor, especially children "in want of suitable clothing to attend the Infant, Sabbath or schools".[10] Emphasising difference from benevolent societies, the Dorcas group aimed to emulate the life of a woman recorded in the New Testament of the Christian Bible. She was Dorcas, a woman of the city of Joppa who did good works without payment, sewing for the needy, attending the sick poor and so on.[11]

The Society's limited resources were intended for those deemed to be deserving of charity and all applicants were vetted to assess their need. Eligible recipients had to be domiciled locally in Hobart Town and environs, including the Cascades, Browns River (now Kingston) and Sandy Bay.[12] This entire locale was divided into sections and allocated to a Dorcas committee member. Each committee member was encouraged to seek subscriptions from the public to fund the Society's work, with one pound providing assistance to four cases. In 1836, the Society paid for a funeral. Money was given to older infirm women, and the Society even paid the cost of passage to Port Phillip, across the Bass Strait, so that wives could join their husbands.[13] In the main, the focus of Dorcas Society was support for pregnant women. In its early years, the Society supplied confinement boxes, containing clean linen and goods, loaned to pregnant women for use during confinement.[14]

Confinement is an archaic term applied to locations where freedom of movement was restricted such as gaols, asylums, and hospitals. In reference to pregnancy, confinement was a period of one month during which women gave

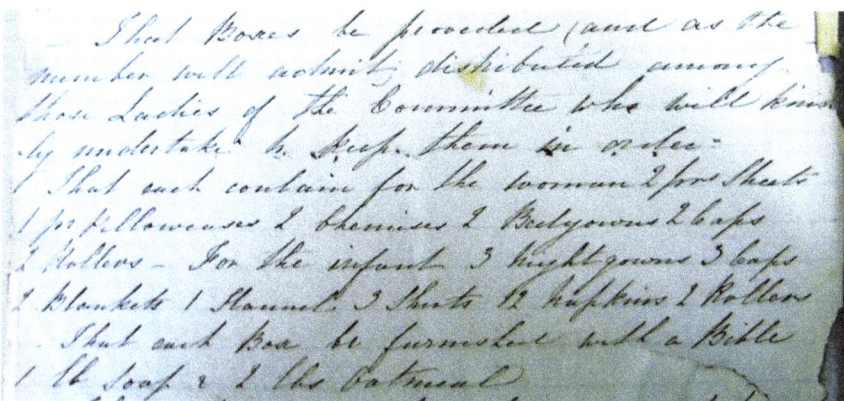

Contents of Dorcas Society confinement boxes/bags as described in the Hobart Town Maternal and Dorcas Society Minutes of Meeting, 31 August 1835.

birth and recovered their health. Also termed the "lying-in" period, the timing of four weeks was a practical matter. In most pregnancies, postpartum blood loss subsides as the uterus contracts gradually. The process takes anywhere from four to six weeks. In the nineteenth century, post-birth blood loss was contained with wads of textiles, not the convenient disposable sanitary padding available today. Thus, the concept of "confinement" ironically freed women from appearing in public until postpartum blood loss had abated.

For destitute women, confinement boxes of the Dorcas Society were a godsend, stocked with items considered necessary for a lying-in, with every item marked "Dorcas Society". A bag within the box contained sheets (2 pairs), pillowcases (1 pair), chemises (2), bedgowns (2), caps (2), rollers/binders (2). Binders were sometimes wound around the abdomen of the mother after delivery, supposedly to encourage the uterus to contract.[15] Supplies for the infant included: nightgowns (3), caps (3), blankets (2), flannel (1), shirts (3), napkins (12), and again rollers (2). Rollers were a form of swaddling cloth, literally rolled around the body of the baby for support. And perhaps indicative that cleanliness was next to godliness, each confinement box held a Bible, 1lb soap and 2lbs oatmeal. Oatmeal could be ground to make gruel for the mother and sometimes babies were fed thin gruel if breast milk was limited. A month after confinement, the box was to be returned "clean, in proper order in which case the infant will be given a set of clothing".[16]

The boxes were distributed by members of the Dorcas committee after cases of distress were identified.[17] Each member kept a quantity of boxes for her designated area. But even this sort of charity had complications. In April 1836, and unfortunately for the intended recipient, the Society recorded that "a confinement box sent to Port Arthur was returned because the commandant did not approve of soldiers' wives being dependent on this assistance".[18] The boxes were loaned on the understanding that they were returned in the condition that they were sent, but sometimes items were missing. Worse than that, in January 1848 the Dorcas Society President, Mrs Nixon, informed the Hobart Town constabulary that some linen marked "Dorcas Society" had been seen in a local pawn shop. Subsequently, senior District Constable J. Symons advised that he'd warned pawnbrokers – anyone caught accepting the Society's boxes and bags would be apprehended and dealt with.[19]

FEMALE MATERNITY ATTENDANTS IN HOBART

In its foundational years, the Hobart Society issued only supplies and money. It did not pay for embodied care. This was a distinct difference from Sydney's Dorcas Society which, from its launch in 1830, ensured that women were attended in their confinements by a midwife.[20] In Hobart, government-appointed midwives worked at the House of Correction, colloquially known as the Female Factory, where Mrs Cato was assistant matron and, in 1835, midwife.[21] The town otherwise had its fair share of educated and experienced midwives.

For instance, Hannah Field arrived in 1821 after accompanying the Mather family from England. Trained at the City of London Lying-in Hospital, Field held its certificate. After marriage to John Barrett in 1823 she continued to practice. Mrs Janet McTavish was a fifty-year-old widow who emigrated from Edinburgh with her daughter and son-in-law. Her first advertisement appeared 17 September 1824, a week after landing in Hobart. It included a glowing testimonial authored by McTavish's midwifery teacher, Dr John Thatcher,[22] founder of the Edinburgh Lying-in Institution for Delivering Poor Married Women at Their Houses.[23] McTavish practiced initially in Elizabeth Street and, after securing a land grant, built a commodious residence called Rosebank at New Town which offered accommodation for women in confinement. In 1836, other pupils of Dr Thatcher, Sarah Barfoot and Janet Miller, commenced practice in Hobart.[24]

These women worked for a living, although what fees they charged is not clear. A Mrs Morrow of Macquarie Street advertised her services as 15s to £1, a lowish fee perhaps because she did not claim education.[25] Colonial Surgeon James Scott's prices for birth attendance were considerable: two guineas in a poor neighbourhood and four guineas in a fashionable suburb like New Town.[26] Such fees were prohibitive for many people, let alone impecunious folk and, in the early 1840s, the Dorcas Society adopted its own form of embodied charity, by paying poor women to "nurse" others, at confinement or cases of illness. This move was made despite a concerted effort by doctors to force all women attending midwifery cases in Van Diemen's Land to hold a licence.

Since 1837, doctors had required a licence to practice under provisions of the *Medical Practitioners Act* (VDL). They were administered by the Governor-appointed Medical Court of Tasmania, colloquially known as the Court of Medical Examiners (CME), made up of seven doctors. The CME's primary purpose was to examine applicants who wished to practise medicine and its various branches, including midwifery.[27] In theory this regulation did not apply to women because they were barred from a university education. But in early 1841, a meeting of the CME posed a question for consideration: "How far can Female Midwifes [sic] Practise without possessing a Certificate of the Board of [Medical] Examiners?"[28] Within weeks, under Section IV of the *Medical Practitioners' Amendment Act 1840* (VDL), the CME approved a bye-law which regulated the "Practice of Midwifery by Females".[29]

Under these new arrangements, female midwives were required to hold a CME-issued "Certificate of Education", supply evidence of "good moral character and of habits of sobriety" and have a "certificate from a physician or surgeon connected with an Institution for the reception and treatment of Lying-in women, or some Lecturer in midwifery of attendance for at least three months upon natural labours".[30] If granted a licence, the midwife was expected to restrict her work to natural labours by which "the Head, Breech, or Lower Extremities" presented and they were to seek assistance of a doctor in cases of haemorrhage, convulsions, or labours lasting longer than 24 hours.[31]

The first of their kind in Australia, these regulations emerged likely owing to competition from educated midwives like those described above, amid Tasmania's worsening financial depression. Whatever its intention, this regulation was spectacularly unsuccessful. Fortunately for the Dorcas Society, it had no effect on its new plan for an embodied form of charity.

EMBODIED CHARITY FOR TRYING TIMES

The first record of someone paid to attend a confinement for the Society was in 1843 when the committee agreed that Mrs Davis, a "poor woman [who] should have seven shillings for attending Mrs Vincent in her confinement".[32] It is possible that this was Mrs Davis of Melville Street near the Rope Walk and of Mr Ray's, baker, of Campbell Street opposite the Penitentiary. When advertising her midwifery credentials in 1833, Davis proudly declared she'd had no disastrous cases in her career, and had recently been in attendance when "three interesting infants" were born to Mrs Ball.[33] Just four years later, reporting of a police matter noted Mrs Davis to be an "old lady" and a midwife with a questionable reputation.[34]

As historian Miranda Morris points out, the records of the Dorcas Society were inconsistent, rarely recording which nurses attended which cases.[35] Descriptors applied to the women and their work range from "nurse" to "midwife" and "nursing" to "attending". The lack of description of cases limits how much can be said of attendants' actual bedside skills and their practices.[36] After Mrs Davis, another woman who featured regularly in the Society's records during the 1840s was [Mrs] Nurse Shingles [sic]. This was likely Elizabeth [Sarah] Shingler, a convict transported on the *Westmoreland* in 1836 and granted a ticket of leave in November 1840.[37]

Sentenced to seven years for shoplifting and stealing handkerchiefs, on arrival in Hobart, Shingler was aged 52, 5'3" tall, with hazel sunken eyes, one with a "cast" indicative of a strabismus or turning.[38] Her conduct record shows that once assigned, she was away without leave on numerous occasions, imprisoned with hard labour, charged with stealing or losing a sheet and reported for insolence.[39] Shingler's home in England was "Wem nr Salisbury". Wem is a market town in Shropshire and it's possible that Shrewsbury was mistaken for Salisbury. Shingler's convict indent notes her occupation as midwife, making her an unusual individual. In Deborah Oxley's landmark study of more than 9,000 convict women transported to New South Wales, only five were named on indents as a midwife.[40]

Shingler was granted a certificate of freedom in 1843.[41] She was first paid by the Dorcas Society in January 1844 being "a poor woman known to the ladies as attentive to the poor in times of sickness".[42] Shingler had assisted two women, Mrs Rogers and Mrs Williamson, receiving ten shillings for her work. During 1844 and 1845, Shingler attended at least 14 cases, amounting to 14 per

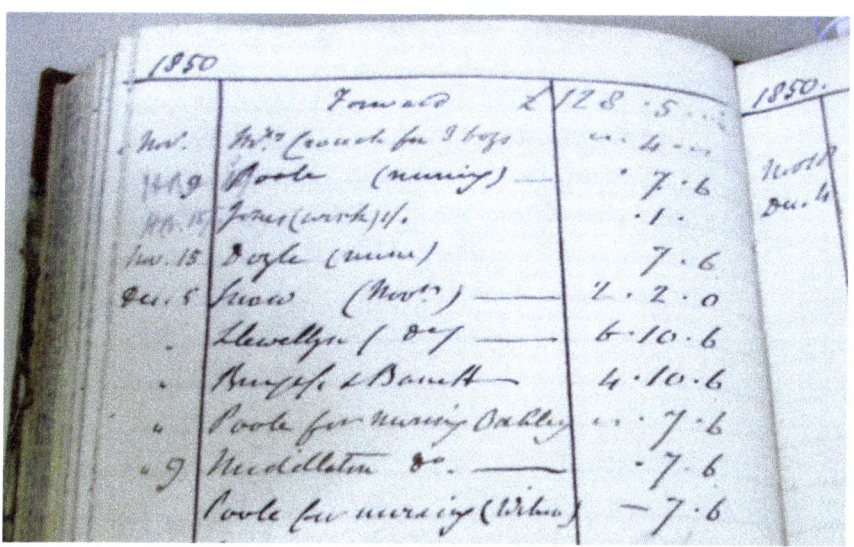

References in the Maternal and Dorcas Society Account Book No. 1 to Mrs Poole paid for nursing cases in November and December 1850.

cent of the total number of confinements cases supported by the Society.[43] But her relationship with the Society was problematic. In April 1845, Shingler was "to be told that she is not to consider herself as employed by the Society – and in future to bring an order from some visiting member authorising her attendance, where she may be employed by the woman".[44] In June 1845, an investigation was ordered when two women were served by Shingler, one at Browns River and the other at Blackmans Bay.[45]

Reading between the lines, it appears that Mrs Shingler began offering her services to women and only telling the Society afterwards. It's also possible she was claiming for attendance that she had not made. One of the committee members, Mrs Turnbull, advocated for Shingler's visitations on different women, but the rest of the Dorcas ladies seemed less unconvinced.[46] They asked Mrs Turnbull to bring one of the confined women before the committee, after recovery from the birth, to vouch for Shingler's attendance.[47] Next came an accusation from a Mrs Whitborne [sic] about Nurse Shingler, in January 1846. The committee resolved to check if women attended by Shingler were satisfied with the nurse, and, in the meantime, withheld her claimed fee. They also decided to dismiss Shingler if the accusation proved true.[48]

The precise nature of Mrs Shingler's faults are unclear. Women certainly asked if Nurse Shingler could attend them, so it's possible that she was spruiking for business, in the hope of generating work for herself.[49] Shingler continued with the Society through 1846 when a total of 48 women received assistance "during the trying time of their confinement".[50] In November 1846, after Shingler sent in a claim for ten shillings, one of the committee was asked to investigate the two cases Shingler claimed to have attended.[51] But by mid-1847, the Dorcas Society's patience was exhausted. The committee disapproved of Shingler's undeclared conduct so much that they decided not to pay her anymore.[52] In January 1849, when Shingler attended on Jane Garrett and applied to the Society for payment, the committee refused her fee given that Shingler was no longer employed by the Society and had not been authorised to attend the case.[53]

Throughout their dealings with Mrs Shingler, the Dorcas Society referred to her as a nurse, even though on her convict indent she nominated her occupation as midwife. It is not clear whether Shingler delivered babies or simply nursed women who had given birth. In the decade beginning 1840, the term "midwife" was recorded only once in reference to an un-named individual, in May 1846.[54] She may have been Mrs Poole, the mainstay of the Dorcas Society's embodied charity into the 1850s. Morris reports that a Mrs Poole was a midwife at the House of Correction in the 1840s, and supplemented her income with engagements for the Dorcas Society, and private cases.[55] As to Nurse Shingler, in 1857 a woman named Sarah Shingler, listed as a general servant born in Shropshire, died at the General Hospital aged 70. It's likely this was the same woman who served the Dorcas Society as Nurse "Elizabeth" Shingler.

In Mrs Davis, Nurse Elizabeth Shingler, and subsequently Mrs Poole, Hobart's Dorcas Society instituted a meaningful form of assistance for respectable poor women during their confinement, a service that continued throughout the nineteenth century until the CME intervened. Historian Joan Brown termed Hobart's Dorcas Society "the grandmother" of Tasmania's charities for its longevity and impact.[56] Without doubt, this powerhouse of women made a palpable difference to the lives of the women judged to be deserving of an embodied charity.

■ ■ ■

ACKNOWLEDGEMENTS

The author wishes to thank staff of the University of Tasmania Archives, Tasmania Parliamentary Library, Archives Office of Tasmanian Archive and Heritage Office.

ENDNOTES

1. *Elliston's Hobart Town Almanack* and *(Ross's) Van Diemen's Land Annual for 1837*, 50.
2. *Bent's News*, April 2, 1836, 2.
3. *Elliston's 1837*, 53.
4. Edward Curr, *Three years residence in Van Diemen's Land: comprising a description of that rising colony, its advantages and prospects, commerce, manners, customs, &c. of its inhabitants, with an account of the bush-rangers, forming a practical guide to emigrants & settlers*, Edinburgh: James Stillie, 1834; Thomas Tegg, *Tegg's handbook for emigrants: containing useful information & practical directions on domestic, mechanical, surgical, medical, and other subjects calculated to increase the comforts, and add to the conveniences of the colonist*, London: George Cowie and Co, 1834.
5. *Trumpeter*, February 14, 1837, 1.
6. *Trumpeter*, June 9, 1837, 3.
7. *Trumpeter*, September 16, 1836, 3.
8. *Colonial Times*, October 27, 1835, 5.
9. Joan C. Brown, "The Development of Social Services in Tasmania 1803–1900", unpublished Masters thesis, University of Tasmania, 1969, 28.
10. Minutes of Meeting, August 31, 1835, Dorcas Society Minute Book 1 (July 9, 1835–December 2, 1846), RS1/2(1), Maternal and Dorcas Society Records 1835–1849, Royal Society of Tasmania Collection, University of Tasmania Library Special and Rare Collections (hereafter Dorcas Society Records).
11. Acts of the Apostles, 9:36–42, *Holy Bible, King James Version*.
12. Minutes of Meeting, July 9, 1835, Dorcas Society Records Minute Book 1, RS1/2(1).
13. Minutes of Meeting, May 3, 1837, Dorcas Society Records Minute Book 1, RS1/2(1).
14. Joyce Purtsch, "The Maternal & Dorcas Society", *Tasmanian Ancestry*, June 1997, 38.
15. Madonna Grehan, "Safely delivered?: Insights into late nineteenth-century Australian maternity care from coronial investigations into maternal deaths", in J. Greenlees & L. Bryder (eds.), *Growing Expectations: Western Childbirth and Medicine since the Nineteenth Century*, (London: Pickering & Chatto Publishers Ltd), 13–29.

16. Minutes of Meeting, August 31, 1835, Dorcas Society Records Minute Book 1, RS1/2(1).
17. Minutes of Meeting, August 31, 1835, Dorcas Society Records Minute Book 1, RS1/2(1).
18. Minutes of Meeting, August 8, 1838, Dorcas Society Records Minute Book 1, RS1/2(1).
19. Letter from Mrs Nixon to Hobart Police, undated, and Notification from Constable Symons to Maternal and Dorcas Society, January 12, 1848, Dorcas Society Records Correspondence RS1/1(1–2).
20. Paul F. Cooper, The Sydney Dorcas Society, "Philanthropists and Philanthropy in Australian Colonial History", available at https://colonialgivers.com/2016/06/24/the-sydney-dorcas-society/#_ednref13 accessed June 19, 2019.
21. Female Convicts Research Centre, List of Employees, available at https://www.femaleconvicts.org.au/convict-institutions/employees/list-of-employees, accessed December 2, 2019.
22. *Hobart Town Gazette and Van Diemen's Land Advertiser*, September 17, 1824, p.1.
23. *The Edinburgh Almanack, or Universal Scots and Imperial Register for 1828*, Edinburgh: Oliver & Boyd, 349.
24. Madonna Grehan, (2012), "Heroes or villains? midwives, nurses, and maternity care in mid-nineteenth-century Australia". *Traffic, Journal of the University of Melbourne Graduate Student Association, Anthology 2012 Women's Edition*, 11–28.
25. *Bent's News and Tasmanian Register*, April 6, 1838, 1.
26. Dusanka Sabic, "Turning Full Circle: A history of midwifery legislation 1901–1928", Unpublished Bachelor of Arts Honours thesis, University of Tasmania, 1986, 19.
27. Minutes of Meeting, February 17, 1841, Minutes of Meetings of the Court of Medical Examiners (hereafter CME Minutes), February 12–November 19, 1901, CB12/1 Archives Office of Tasmania, Hobart.
28. CME Minutes, March 4, 1841.
29. CME Minutes, April 7, 1841.
30. CME Minutes, April 7, 1841.
31. CME Minutes, April 7, 1841.
32. Minutes of Meeting, September 6, 1843, Dorcas Society Minute Book 1, RS1/2(1).
33. *Colonial Times*, November 26, 1833, 1.
34. *Colonial Times*, April 18, 1837, 8.
35. Miranda Morris, *Placing Women: A methodology for the identification, interpretation and promotion of the heritage of women in Tasmania* (Hobart: Office of the Status of Women, State Government of Tasmania, 1996), 57. The Dorcas Society records contain a surprising level of detail about families who received relief such as: names, addresses, and conditions which delivered distress (broken thighs from industrial accidents, hospitalisation of husbands and so on).

36. Madonna Grehan, "Professional Aspirations and Consumer Expectations: Nurses, Midwives and Women's Health", Unpublished PhD thesis, The University of Melbourne, 2009, 245.
37. *Hobart Town Courier and Van Diemen's Land Gazette*, December 1, 1840, 2.
38. Description of Elizabeth Shingler, Principal Superintendent of Convicts, Description lists of female convicts arriving in VDL per: *Majestic*, January 22, 1839, *Newgrove*, March 27, 1835, *Nautilus*, August 27, 1838, *Westmoreland*, December 3, 1836, *William Bryan*, October 23, 1833, *Platina*, October 22, 1837, Archives Office of Tasmania, CON/19/1/14 p.456, available at https://stors.tas.gov.au/CON19-1-14$init=CON19-1-14p247, accessed December 1, 2019.
39. Elizabeth Shingler, Conduct Record, Principal Superintendent of Convicts, Alphabetical Record Book of female convicts arriving in VDL S–Y 1836, CON/40/1/10 p.456, available at https://stors.tas.gov.au/CON40-1-10$init=CON40-1-10p8, accessed December 1, 2019.
40. Deborah Oxley, "Convict Maids", Unpublished PhD thesis, University of New South Wales, 1991, 159.
41. *Hobart Town Courier and Van Diemen's Land Gazette*, June 2, 1843, 4.
42. Minutes of Meeting, January 3, 1844, Dorcas Society Records Minute Book 1, RS1/2(1).
43. *Annual Reports for 1844 and 1845*, Dorcas Society Records Reports, RS1/10.
44. Minutes of Meeting, April 10, 1845, Dorcas Society Records Minute Book 1, RS1/2(1).
45. Minutes of Meeting, June 4, 1845, Dorcas Society Records Minute Book 1, RS1/2(1).
46. Minutes of Meeting, July 2, 1845, Dorcas Society Records Minute Book 1, RS1/2(1).
47. Minutes of Meeting, July 2, 1845, Dorcas Society Records Minute Book 1, RS1/2(1).
48. Minutes of Meeting, January 7, 1846, Dorcas Society Records Minute Book 1, RS1/2(1).
49. Minutes of Meeting, November 5, 1845, Dorcas Society Records Minute Book 1, RS1/2(1).
50. *Courier*, February 20, 1847, 4.
51. Minutes of Meeting, November 4, 1847, Dorcas Society Records Minute Book 2 (January 6, 1847–January 3, 1849), RS1/2 (2).
52. Minutes of Meeting, August 4, 1847, Dorcas Society Minute Book 2, RS1/2 (2).
53. Minutes of Meeting, January 3, 1849, Dorcas Society Minute Book 3 (January 3, 1849–May 1, 1850), RS1/2 (3).
54. Accounts for May 1846, Dorcas Society Records Account Book November 1836–December 1853, RS1/5/1.
55. Morris, 58.
56. Brown, 28.

The original Gordon-below-Franklin dispute: Beattie, BHP and Marble Cliffs

NIC HAYGARTH

Tasmania's lower Gordon River has been saved twice. In the summer of 1982–83, a conservationist blockade was staged to protest and publicise the Tasmanian State Government's intention to dam the lower Gordon as part of a hydro-electric power development. The dam would have flooded not just kilometres of the Gordon River but much of the magnificent, wild Franklin River, inundating the Aboriginal heritage cave Kutikina and other untold, undiscovered archaeological sites. It took a High Court ruling to stop the dam. The Federal Government, it ruled, could enforce its right to legislate on any issue in order to fulfil its responsibilities under an international treaty, in this case, the UNESCO Convention for the Protection of the World Cultural and Natural Heritage.[1]

This was effectively a replay of an earlier conservation battle which had long been forgotten. Not only did people power triumph on the lower Gordon River almost 70 years before the Gordon-below-Franklin Dam Blockade, but it did so by swaying a pro-development premier – a feat of which the Blockaders could only dream in the summer of 1982–83. The subject of the 1914 battle was karst – a 40-metre-high bank of limestone known as the Marble Cliffs (now Champ Cliff).[2]

Limestone extends for up to 17km along the lower Gordon River.[3] Convicts from the nearby Macquarie Harbour penal station based at Sarah Island were the first to quarry limestone in this area in 1822–33.[4] A convict-era

The Marble Cliffs, Gordon River, Tasmania.
Stephen Spurling III, courtesy of Stephen Hiller

kiln, later reused by a mining company, can still be found at Limekiln Reach.[5] Caves were probably discovered in the limestone karst during lime burning or logging operations along the lower Gordon in the convict era.

The culling of Huon pine on the Gordon River, and later the advent of mining in the Mount Lyell district, gradually made the Gordon River accessible to would-be limestone quarriers. In 1886 there were efforts to sell Tasmanian "marble" in London, where it was hoped it would compete with Sicilian marble. Two syndicates fought for possession of the Gordon River's Marble Cliffs about 25km upstream of the mouth of the Gordon River.[6] Four years later, polished samples of this limestone exhibited in the mineralogical exhibition at Crystal Palace in London were said to be especially suitable for use in churches, both for altar pieces and flooring.[7]

There was quality. Was there quantity? Government geologist Alexander Montgomery said there was not enough "marble" at the Marble Cliffs to make a quarry viable.[8] Broken Hill Proprietary Ltd (BHP) director Daniel Griffith held a different opinion, claiming that the Marble Cliffs represented "one of the most admirable fluxes in existence".[9]

Evening, the piner's hut, Gordon River, Tasmania.
Stephen Spurling III, courtesy of Stephen Hiller

It was at this time that the Hobart photographer John Watt Beattie (1859–1930) made his first trip to the West Coast.[10] Beattie, the most important figure in 19th and early 20th century Tasmanian tourism and conservation, was not one of those "wilderness" photographers who excluded people from his photos. He worked in the aesthetic of the sublime, typically depicting a man awestruck or at least wonderstruck by God's immense creation, nature. Beattie was himself sometimes transfixed by nature, declaring that, "I love the bush, and nothing gives me greater delight than to stand on top of some high land and look out on a wild array of our mountain giants. I am struck dumb, but oh, my soul sings!"[11]

As a passionate amateur historian, Beattie also celebrated and helped de-stigmatise Tasmania's convict past.[12] No other place suited Beattie quite like the West Coast, where frenetic enterprise, wondrous scenery and brutal penal history were fused.

In the mid-1890s the Mount Lyell Copper Mine prompted the last 19th century Australia-wide mining boom. The mine, worth more than £4 million in

Gordon River, West Coast, Tasmania.
Stephen Spurling III

1897, was the powerhouse of the Tasmanian economy.[13] Sensibly, West Coasters tried to diversify economically by placing tourism alongside mining. To this end, Strahan merchant John Ware subtitled his 1908 tourist guidebook *Strahan: Macquarie Harbour* both "the commercial port of the western mineral fields" and "unsurpassed for scenic grandeur and as a health resor". The book included

Ware's poem *The Gordon,* which described the river "rippling on unruffled, past fairy grottoes and caves", in the fantasy mode fashionable at the time.[14]

Gordon River cruises were then an expensive indulgence. Some tourists baulked at the minimum of £5 per day required to charter a launch or motorboat at Strahan. The Marble Cliffs were said to be one of the three gems of the river, along with Sir John Falls and Butler Island. These featured in photos, postcards, lettercards and lantern slides which advertised Gordon River cruises.[15] Most of these photos were taken by two superb landscape photographers, J. W. Beattie and Stephen Spurling III.

J. W. BEATTIE'S CAMPAIGN FOR A GORDON RIVER NATIONAL PARK

It is easy to imagine that Beattie and Spurling's magnificent photos of the lower Gordon and King Rivers were persuasive elements in the creation of 100-metre-wide reserves along the banks of these rivers in 1908.[16] Tim Bonyhady has discussed how Beattie, a frequent lantern lecturer, campaigned to have the 1908 Gordon River Reserve extended.[17] Beattie believed at this time that Tasmania was not yet ready to accept reservation of an area simply because of its intrinsic qualities, rather, that a national park needed to be justified on purely economic grounds. He therefore asserted that the Gordon River was worthless to timber cutters, to miners, to farmers and to settlers. Attracting the tourist pound, he implied, was its only chance of redemption.[18] The same rationale was used by other campaigners for two early Tasmanian national parks, those at Mount Field and Cradle Mountain–Lake St Clair.[19]

THE PROPOSAL TO MINE THE MARBLE CLIFFS

What hasn't been pointed out previously is that Beattie's lantern lecture campaign was a failure, and that his proposed Gordon River National Park faced a battle that went to the core of his belief system. The genesis of this battle was in the connection between the Mount Lyell Mining and Railway Company and BHP. It was Bowes Kelly and other BHP directors who bought the Mount Lyell Gold Mine and turned it into a copper mine.[20] In 1914, at a time when BHP planned to expand into steel manufacturing at Newcastle, Kelly, now a director of both companies, appears to have reminded BHP of the potential of the Marble Cliffs to provide smelting flux. BHP applied to lease the site. The company believed that shipping from western Tasmania to Newcastle would be economical if a bar across the Gordon River was removed, the limestone being back loaded on vessels delivering coke and coal to Mount Lyell and other West Coast mines.[21]

The plan to quarry limestone was popular as an employment initiative on the West Coast, but there was less support for destruction of one of the pillars of Gordon River tourism.[22] West Coast (Wilmot House of Assembly electorate) member Edward Mulcahy was among those who suggested that limestone could be hacked invisibly from the back of the Marble Cliffs deposit.[23] BHP's proposed lease, however, reached right to the water's edge, leaving no doubt of its intention to violate the existing reserve by mining the cliffs' river-side face. John Ware, gusher of Gordon River poetry, now dismissed the Marble Cliffs as "puny" and "disinteresting", merely the turning-around point for cruise services.[24] Some justified the scheme by its creation of jobs and on the "more accessible" social justice argument: by providing accommodation, a small mining settlement at the Marble Cliffs would make Gordon River tourism cheaper, opening it to the masses.[25] Such justifications would become staples of development proposals in Tasmania.

Elsewhere in the state, the plan was greeted with disgust. In Launceston, *Weekly Courier* editor Frederick Pritchard pleaded for the Gordon's preservation for future generations.[26] In Hobart, *Mercury* editor William Henry Simmons expressed "horror and anger" at the proposed "vandalism".[27] One protestor offered Junee Cave limestone to the developers as a trade-off for the Marble Cliffs.[28] Beattie stepped out of the cover of economics forever by attacking the mining scheme as "unpatriotic" and "the thin edge of utilitarianism". He declared that the Gordon River should be a "sacred reserve for all time", and blasted the "ridiculous" existing riverbank reservation.[29] Beattie was a member of the Tasmanian Tourists' Association, which backed his call to refuse the BHP mining lease.[30]

JOHN EARLE ADJUDICATES

The premier of the time, John Earle (1865–1932), had developed an interest in politics in his 20s while working as a humble blacksmith at the remote Lucy Spur Gold Mine, above the middle reaches of the Pieman River on the West Coast.[31] Later, on the Zeehan silver field, Earle and his future minister for mines James Ogden, were prominent figures in the Amalgamated Miners Association.[32]

Mining was in Earle's blood, and in the shadow of World War I his traditional supporters in mining communities expected government relief. While Mount Lyell, a producer of a strategic metal, sailed through the war, most Tasmanian mining was brought to a standstill by the closure of the European metal markets. Co-operative arrangements with miners enabled some work to continue at the Tasmania Gold Mine and the Mount Bischoff Tin Mine.[33] The Earle Government also established the Electrolytic Zinc plant in Hobart to save the zinc that was being discarded on West Coast mine dumps.[34] The generation of hydro-electric power for this plant effectively marked the beginning of hydro-industrialisation, a dogmatic policy of Tasmanian governments into the 1980s.

Earle was a pro-development premier, but not a rapacious one. His Labor government in the years 1914–16 also took control of tourism, passed more effective conservation legislation (the *Scenery Preservation Act*, 1915) and established Tasmania's first national parks at Freycinet and Mount Field. These measures reflected a growing appreciation of the environment in Tasmania. Perhaps those years of working in "nature primeval" on the middle reaches of the beautiful Pieman, a river of similar grandeur to the Gordon, had worked on Earle's soul. Under pressure from tourist associations, newspaper editors, the high-profile Beattie and the general populace, Earle decided to refuse the BHP application. His explanation for the decision—for which he claimed sole responsibility – suggests that it was not politically convenient to admit that he had intervened in the name of nature preservation. He told Parliament that, "There was no indication that a genuine industry was likely to be established [at the Marble Cliffs] ... he looked upon the scheme as a wild cat one. He considered it was doomed to failure, and would only result in the destruction of beautiful scenery."[35]

The logic of this statement seems to have been lost on Earle's own cabinet members: to accuse the highly capitalised BHP, of all companies, of a "wild cat" operation was very surprising. Moreover, why, after making that accusation, did he endorse a BHP limestone quarry at Melrose, about 15 kilometres from the nearest port in north-western Tasmania?

The West Coast took the news badly.[36] BHP, however, was not completely fazed by the decision because the company was welcomed with open arms at Melrose. There was little parliamentary opposition to the *Don-Melrose Tramway Act*, 1915, which enabled the Tasmanian Government to publicly fund the tramway bringing BHP's smelting flux out to the wharf at Devonport.[37] Renouncing any interest in the Gordon, BHP operated its Melrose quarry from 1915 until 1947.[38]

A DATE WITH A DAM

Ominously, BHP general manager Guillaume Delprat envisaged another practical use of the lower Gordon besides limestone extraction. He pronounced the river ideal for hydro-electric power generation.[39] Beattie's Gordon River national park (the Franklin–Gordon Wild Rivers National Park) would not be gazetted until 1981 – and its proclamation would not prevent a second Gordon-below-Franklin battle. Artists and activists had a date with a dam. While the tussle with BHP was by then long forgotten, the use of striking scenic images to sway opinion and garner support was now central to conservation campaigns. One photograph in particular, Peter Dombrovskis' *Morning mist, Rock Island Bend,* has come to represent the successful protest against the Gordon-below-Franklin Dam, crystallising the philosophy of ecological protection for an international audience.

Beattie would have been amazed and thrilled by the triumph of his own medium in the service of his most passionate cause. Saving the lower Gordon was, as he predicted in 1908, a case of "the proverbial drop of water on the stone" – but one image on a broadsheet and a television screen had the power to shatter the political fundament.[40]

■ ■ ■

ENDNOTES

1. Kevin Kiernan, "The Impact of the World Heritage Convention on the Management of Karst in Tasmania", *Proceedings of the Cave Management in Australasia 8 Conference* (A.C.K.M.A., Punakaiki, New Zealand, 1989), 92–117.
2. Karst refers to a type of landform characterised by the dissolution of carbonate rocks such as limestone, dolomite and magnesite.
3. Kevin Kiernan, *An Atlas of Tasmanian Karst*, Research Report 10 (Tasmanian Forest Research Council Inc., Hobart, 1995), 2, 32.
4. Hamish Maxwell-Stewart, *Closing Hells Gates: The death of a convict station* (Allen & Unwin, Crows Nest, N.S.W., 2008), 31–32.
5. J. W. Beattie, quoted in "The Wild West Coast", *Examiner*, July 14, 1908, 6.
6. "By Electric Telegraph", *Mercury*, November 26, 1886, 3.
7. "A New Tasmanian Industry", *Mercury*, October 1, 1890, 3.
8. Alexander Montgomery, "Report on the Black Marble Found on the Gordon River, Macquarie Harbour", 1890; in "Application R. W. [sic] O'Brien Marble Cliffs–Gordon River", AB948/1/105 114 (TAHO).

9. "Mining Intelligence", *Launceston Examiner*, October 8, 1891, 3.
10. Nic Haygarth, *Booming Tasmania: How the Anson/Beattie Photographic Studio sold the island and itself 1880–1901* (State Library of Tasmania Research Fellowship Report) (the author, Perth, Tas.), 2008, 64.
11. J. W. Beattie, quoted in "Death of Mr J. W. Beattie", *Mercury*, June 25, 1930, 7.
12. David Young, *Making Crime Pay: the Evolution of Convict Tourism in Tasmania* (Tasmanian Historical Research Association, Hobart, 1996).
13. Geoffrey Blainey, *The Peaks of Lyell* (Melbourne University Press, 1954), 79–80.
14. John Ware, *Strahan: Macquarie Harbour*, (the author, Strahan, 1908), 9.
15. The so-called "magic lantern" projected images on glass slides. Magic lantern shows were like early slide presentations.
16. "Correspondence re Deputation from the Tasmanian Tourists Association re Mineral Leases at Marble Cliffs on the Gordon River", 1914, TRE5/1/1865 (TAHO).
17. Tim Bonyhady, *The Colonial Earth*, (Melbourne University Press, 2000), 102–12.
18. J. W. Beattie, "Notes on the River Gordon and on the Need for Reservation of Land Along its Banks", *Papers and Proceedings of the Royal Society of Tasmania of Tasmania*, 1908, 35.
19. William Crooke, letter to Secretary for Lands, September 4, 1913, "Mount Field National Park Board Correspondence: ANM Joint Committee", AA579/1/3 (TAHO); "Suggested National Park", *Mercury*, September 16, 1913, 4; "The Proposed New National Reserve", *Mercury*, August 8, 1921, 4.
20. Blainey, *The Peaks of Lyell*, 57–58.
21. A. P. C. Ross, letter to Edward Mulcahy, 1915, in "Application R. W. [sic] O'Brien Marble Cliffs–Gordon River", AB948/1/105 114 (TAHO).
22. "Gordon River Scenery: Protest Against Destruction", *Mercury*, June 6, 1914, 3; "Queenstown: Mount Lyell Tourist Association", *Zeehan and Dundas Herald*, June 6, 1914, 4; "Queenstown Municipal Council", *Zeehan and Dundas Herald*, June 15, 1914, 4.
23. Edward Mulcahy, "The Marble Cliffs, Gordon River", *Mercury*, May 28, 1914, 7.
24. John Ware, "Marble Cliffs, Gordon River", *Daily Post*, June 4, 1914, 4.
25. Ben Watkins, letter to J. E. Ogden, 1914, in "Application R. W. [sic] O'Brien Marble Cliffs–Gordon River", AB948/1/105 114 (TAHO); "O. E. W.", "Marble Cliffs", *Mercury*, June 19, 1914, 2.
26. Frederick Pritchard, "A Threatened National Asset", *Weekly Courier*, June 4, 1914, 25.
27. William Henry Simmons, "The Marble Cliffs", *Mercury*, May 28, 1914, 4.
28. R. Marriott junior, "The Gordon River", *Mercury*, June 4, 1914, 6.
29. J. W. Beattie; quoted in "Marble Cliffs Threatened", *Weekly Courier*, May 28, 1914, 25.
30. "The Gordon River: Marble Cliffs Question", *Mercury*, June 18, 1914, 6.
31. Mark Ireland, *Pioneering on North-east Coast and West Coast of Tasmania*, *Examiner* Office, Launceston, c1913, 34.
32. Patrick Howard, *The Zeehan El Dorado: A history of Zeehan* (Mount Heemskirk Books, Blackmans Bay, 2006), 295–96.

33. Glyn Roberts, *Metal Mining in Tasmania 1804 to 1914: How the government helped shape the mining industry* (Bokprint and Fullers Bookshop, Launceston, 2007), 285; Mount Bischoff Tin Mining Company directors' meeting minutes, August 27, 1914, 423; September 8, 1914, 430–31 and September 9, 1914, 432, NS911/15 (TAHO).
34. W. A. Townsley, *Tasmania from Colony to Statehood 1803–1945* (St David's Park, Hobart, 1991), 268.
35. "Melrose Tramway Bill", *Zeehan and Dundas Herald*, February 1, 1915, 1.
36. "A Contrast in Policy", *Zeehan and Dundas Herald*, January 26, 1915, 2; Zeehan and Districts Development Committee, letter to J. E. Ogden January 15, 1915, in "Application R. W. [sic] O'Brien Marble Cliffs–Gordon River", AB948/1/105 114 (TAHO).
37. "Melrose Lime Deposits: Building of the Railway", *Mercury*, 8 April, 1915, 5.
38. Faye Gardam, *Sawdust, Sails and Sweat: A history of the River Don Settlement, North-west Coast, Tasmania* (the author, Port Sorell, 1996), 68–70.
39. "Queenstown: the Gordon River", *Zeehan and Dundas Herald*, April 10, 1914, 4.
40. "The Gordon River", *Mercury*, July 14, 1908, 6.

Beware of Mrs Browne

FIONA MacFARLANE

On December 1, 1861, newly appointed Governor Colonel, Thomas Gore Browne, his 32-year-old wife Harriet and their four young children arrived in Hobart Town, Tasmania. Harriet, an avid diarist and aspiring novelist, was less than impressed by what she observed upon entering her new home, Government House on the Queen's Domain. She wrote:

> The situation looked bare & staring with no trees near & yellow hay all round. A very shabby looking butler (ours now) opened the door & turning to what I knew was the drawing-room door, we met Sir Henry, an insignificant Jewish-looking round about little man. Lady Y[oung] was awaiting us in the library – & was a featherbed in lilac muslin. They are neither at all distinguished or aristocratic, but she has self-confidence & self-appreciation – great qualities – no doubt.

Harriet had every reason to feel deflated. As a child growing up at her family's ancestral mansion, Craigie House in Ayrshire, Scotland, she fantasised about becoming an Earl's wife and leading society in the country.[1] Harriet's marriage, therefore, to a Lieutenant-Colonel in the British army on half-pay and 22 years her senior was not a promising start, nor was her father's[2] initial opposition to the union. It wasn't until Thomas' appointment as Governor of St Helena[3] that her father yielded, and the couple wed in June 1851. Shortly after, Harriet, Thomas and Fred Steward (Thomas' cousin and private secretary) moved to St Helena, remaining there until August 1855, when Thomas or "Gore" as Harriet addressed him in her diaries, was sent to govern New Zealand, a relatively new colony, but generally considered a desirable posting. Doubtless,

Harriet Louisa Browne, 1868.
NS655/1/262, Tasmanian Archives

Harriet believed that Thomas' career trajectory was ascending, as evidenced by her diary entry of September 1, 1855. Espying a rare double rainbow from the ship near Auckland, she wrote, "A beautiful double rainbow seemed a promising omen and I never felt so excited or joyous in my life."[4]

Thomas' NZ governorship began smoothly, and thanks largely to Harriet's affability, generosity and constant need for amusement and companionship, Government House in Auckland became the epicentre of social life in New Zealand and was constantly filled with members of the Auckland elite, attending lavish dinner parties, balls and other gatherings. By 1856, however, things had begun to sour, with several commentators, including Thomas' own Colonial

Government House, Hobart Town, 1861.
*Alfred Abbott, SD_ILS: 132328, Abbott Album item 33,
W. L. Crowther Library, SLT*

Secretary, Dr Andrew Sinclair, questioning the Browne's extravagance. A bemused Harriet thought it "very absurd to think of the sacrifices required to live upon what at home is considered a good income",[5] and expressed her preference for living like, "a Governor in the large house, seeing people and keeping up a position", rather than living "like small people in a cottage with 4 servants".[6]

In 1859, Thomas, or Colonel Browne, as he was frequently called in New Zealand, allowed the sale of disputed Maori land in Waitera, in the province of Taranaki, to accommodate thousands of new European settlers, a policy that eventually resulted in the outbreak of war between imperial troops and indigenous Maori. While many white settlers supported Thomas' use of force against Maori resistance, Thomas faced vehement opposition by prominent members of New Zealand society, including politicians, judges, journalists and Anglican church ministers. They believed his actions were unjust, illegal and morally reprehensible and used their extensive networks in England to influence both British public opinion and the Colonial Office to replace him as Governor. The Gore Brownes started losing friends.

Despite Harriet's own assertion that "she didn't like meddling in politics as it was dangerous",[7] she assisted Thomas with speech writing, reading and formulating despatches and, in a desperate letter-writing campaign to friends and relatives back in Britain. One onlooker, Jane Maria Atkinson,[8] wrote that Harriet "really governs the country as much as the governor, for he does nothing and writes nothing without consulting her first".[9] Harriet also wrote a lengthy pamphlet that outlined the origins and progress[10] of the conflict in Taranaki, and organised contentious social gatherings at Government House, using what she called "ear-wigging" tactics to influence wavering politicians and their wives. These actions displeased many eminent politicians,[11] who warned her to stop interfering. One gentleman even approached Harriet's lady's maid, Burty, telling her that although he liked the Governor and Harriett for their "kindness to the poor at St Helena", he had been warned "beware of Mrs Browne".[12]

Political volatility and criticism of Thomas' governorship continued to mount, and by October 1860 alarming rumours circulated that Auckland was facing imminent attack by members of the Maori resistance. Advisors also warned Thomas that the threat of his assassination was very real, although Harriet was less convinced. She was, however, increasingly worried about his future as an administrator in public office and acknowledged that a formal rebuke, premature dismissal, demotion or recall to England would almost certainly destroy his career, their reputation and their financial prospects. In July 1861, the Colonial Office in London replaced Thomas with former New Zealand Governor Sir George Grey,[13] and while Thomas escaped official censure and recall, he was demoted to govern the almost bankrupt former convict colony of Tasmania. Harriet received this news with a mixture of relief and mortification. Thomas was still employed and could support their burgeoning family, but she construed his transfer to Tasmania as a public vote of no confidence.

Prior to leaving New Zealand in late October 1861, Thomas and Harriet shared Government House with Thomas' successor, Sir George, and Harriet was beguiled by his intellect, ambition and charisma, a fact that did not escape Thomas' attention:

> Gore says I would worship Sir G if I were his wife because he can do & does so much, but if he is dishonest (which is mean) it would destroy the effect his greatness would produce on my mind.[14]

Later, as the Brownes set sail for Australia aboard the Henry Fernie, Harriet lamented:

> We had left N Zealand & had no longer any influence either for good or evil on coming events – added to this there was along with great admiration for Sir George a sore feeling towards him – as to the man who would have all the honor I should have ardently craved for Gore – now my chief desire is to awake his ambition for the future or at least a desire to be of use in his new sphere; as

> yet he seems to think more of the past than of the future & rather throws cold water on my castles for Tasmania – The place seems going down in the world.[15]

After spending a month in Sydney,[16] the family arrived in Hobart Town, and in contrast to the elation Harriet felt when she sailed into Auckland Harbour in 1855, Harriet was now apprehensive and subdued. Her husband's career was on a downward trajectory, she was uncertain about the reception they would receive in the colony, and in consequence of the colony's staggering debts,[17] funding for the new Tasmanian Governor's establishment had been severely reduced.[18] But uppermost in Harriet's mind were her doubts about Thomas' management of Maori affairs – policies and actions that had resulted in bloodshed.

> It is clearly by Gore's act that this whole sad war began, now if by any chance that act was a wrong one (which public opinion now seems to say it was), who is to blame? I am sure Gore acted to the best of his ability & I am also sure that in every step he asked for wisdom – so what could he have done more?[19]

New Zealand historian, Professor Charlotte Macdonald, argued that by late 1861 Harriet was wondering whether "she may have led her husband to a wrong set of resolutions. In her reviewing, rehearsing, and scrutinising of her judgement, she was attempting to appraise her own actions. If these were errors of judgement, were they her own lapses or deficiencies? Was she also standing accused by history as having acted illegally or unjustly?"[20]

If the following diary entry is any indication, Harriet *was* plagued by guilt and self-doubt about her involvement in New Zealand politics:

> We ... returned to the factory[21] where there are 120 criminals – rather horrid – only 4 of them came out free. I saw a woman who scolded a child to death. I did not speak to many, not knowing how bad criminals they were. I daresay I am as bad ...[22]

To compound matters, New Zealand newspaper articles continued to impugn Thomas' character as former Governor, unsettling the Gore Brownes for the next few years:

> When we came home I fell upon an article copied in the Advertiser about N[ew] Z[ealand] affairs – it said how fearful a verdict would

Sir G[eorge]'s success pronounce upon his predecessor if it showed that a better administration & a little kindness were all that were required to avert the war. This knocked me down, I was cross & frantic all evening & woke oppressed.[23]

It was perhaps this guilt, as well as a sincere desire to be useful, that led Harriet to charity work in Tasmania. Unlike her predecessor, Lady Young, Harriet spent much time visiting orphans, hospital patients and impoverished residents, often reading to them, giving them money and bags of food grown in the grounds of Government House. She even contended with naughty and recalcitrant children while teaching at several ragged schools. Harriet was proud of the contribution she made to benevolent causes in Hobart Town and later observed:

> The dignity of Govt House was being restored by a liberality, very unlike the meanness & shabbiness which got the Youngs into such disrepute.[24]

During this time, Harriet received an unwelcome visit from Miss Mary Gellibrand, a friend of the former Tasmanian Governor's wife, Lady Augusta Young. Mary explained to Harriet that, "It was a very bold thing to be the friend of the Govr's wife,"[25] that she had personally lost friends and created jealously from this relationship, that Harriet would need "thick skin" to navigate her way through the pitfalls of her position, and that Lady Young had recently written to the ladies of Hobart Town, encouraging them to support Harriet and to try and like Harriet as much as they had liked Lady Young.

"Thank her for nothing," Harriet wrote. "I will soon make them all like me better than they ever did her."[26]

And so, the indomitable Harriet forged ahead with her new life. She admired her luxurious new house on the Domain, with its vast grounds and sweeping river views, and unlike Thomas' posting in New Zealand, where Harriet was preoccupied with political machinations, she could spend quality time with her children. She also enjoyed the "delicious climate", and her travels around Hobart Town, unlike Thomas who preferred to stay at home.

"I quarrelled with Gore because he showed his usual inclination to shirk doing much & talked about its not being a Governor's duty to explore."[27]

On February 12, 1862, much to Thomas' dismay, Harriet and Thomas embarked on a two-month vice-regal tour of northern Tasmania, the first of many journeys around Tasmania. The purpose of this travelling was to familiarise themselves with the colony and its network of powerful and influential colonists. Being an experienced hostess back in New Zealand and at St Helena, Harriet was a skilful conversationalist and made friends easily, an important step on the road to becoming more popular than Lady Young. These friends included Robert Quayle Kermode and his wife Emily, from Mona Vale estate, near Ross, Sir Richard Dry and his wife Clara, of Quamby estate, near Hagley, and Port Arthur Commandant James Boyd and his daughter Marion[28] (despite their propensity to joke about the freshly landed prisoners wearing their "sear and yellow leaf"[29] clothing and the clattering of their chains). Harriet meticulously and evocatively chronicled her excursions, describing scenery, public institutions, country estates she stayed at and noteworthy characters she encountered along the way, including several Tasmanian Aborigines, such as Truganini, William Lanne and Bessy Clark:

> The natives, from speaking our language, are much more amusing than Maories. There were 4 women & one man & they sat & looked at the ladies & made remarks quite cheerfully. Bessie shouted with delight when I told her I would ask her to the ball.[30]

Harriet also enjoyed camping in the Tasmanian wilderness with various well-known personages, including naturalist Ronald Campbell Gunn, and members of the Langdon and Sharland families. Together, they stoically survived violent storms, a leaking boat and flea-infested beds. The Walker family of Rhodes estate, near Perth, also received particular attention in Harriet's diary as they shared haunting tales of family members who had died tragically, including 15-year-old Selina who, in 1849, drowned in the South Esk River and was ingloriously removed from the water by grappling irons attached to her long hair.[31]

Wherever Harriet went, she interrogated new acquaintances about former Tasmanian vice-regal identities, in an attempt, perhaps, not to repeat their mistakes:

> [Mr Innes] told me Sir J[ohn] Franklin was no better than a child, that, at a council upon disturbances on Sunday, he told a little story of how he had met a little boy playing marbles & asked him to desist. Mr I[nnes] says his friends gave him his character & that Lady Franklin was a woman of great talent but wanting in judgement & that it was to efface his civil

disgrace that she drove him to the North Pole. She was too
blue & women did not like her.³²

Despite Harriet's best efforts though, she *did* blunder, destroying her credibility with numerous society ladies of Hobart Town. During an "at home" at Government House on December 30, 1862, Harriet invited politician, businessman and newspaper proprietor John Davies and his wife to the festivities, despite hearing unsubstantiated rumours that he was an ex-convict (an allegation that the Attorney General himself couldn't prove). Davies was also on Lady Young's old guest list, convincing Harriet of his suitability to attend social events at Government House. After this function, 14 eminent families, including the Gellibrands, Allports and Crowthers, disgusted by Davies' appearance, requested that their names be removed from Harriet's guest lists and organised, "opposition parties to which no one going to Govt House would be invited".³³ By employing this tactic, they forewent countless official functions at Government House, including dinner parties with naval officers from the HMS *Orpheus*, the ill-fated flagship of the Australian squadron, wrecked near Auckland in February 1863, killing 189 men, and the Duke of Penthievre's,³⁴ stopover in Hobart Town in October 1866.³⁵

Not surprisingly, in January 1868, when the Duke of Edinburgh arrived in Hobart Town, the opposition families ended their boycott of Government House. On January 6, 1868, 24-year-old Prince Alfred, the Duke of Edinburgh, along with a cohort of friends and "advisors", arrived in Hobart Town per HMS *Galatea*, a frigate Alfred commanded. This 12-day visit was part of the calamitous Royal tour of Australia that terminated unexpectedly in Sydney after Alfred was shot and severely wounded by an Irish would-be assassin, James O'Farrell. While author Steve Harris only alluded to the Prince's Tasmanian tour in his recent book,³⁶ Harriet wrote innumerable pages about the royal party's boisterous and ungentlemanly antics, including them denigrating people they didn't like, being unpunctual or failing to attend official events, and during frequent bouts of drunken revelry, disclosing personal information [verbatim] about members of the Royal Family:

> We had … an account of the dreary dinners at Windsor where the Queen, having dined at 2 gobbles & there is no conversation, but, "Oh yes, your Majesty," everything else being said in whispers. He says her life must be schockingly [sic] dull, but that she is so shy

> she will never come forward again. But people know nothing of it who say she will abdicate. Nothing is so unlikely - she will stick to the throne till the last – he says she behaves very badly to the Prince of W[ales] but is very fond of the Princess.[37]

Unlike Alfred's stay in Melbourne, where he abandoned the Victorian Governor, Viscount John Manners Sutton (labelled "old snuffy" by Alfred[38]) to live in a brothel (and allegedly impregnating a prostitute), Alfred genuinely liked Harriet and did not renounce her. Despite Harriet's polite and friendly exterior, she didn't respect the prince, secretly regarding him as selfish and inconsiderate. These opinions were reinforced when Alfred left Hobart Town, sending all the bills he had incurred during the Royal tour to Government House. Harriet wrote:

> Certainly, his cruise has been a dire mistake & will create mutual dislike & contempt. I don't think any qualities on his part could have made it a success.[39]

Contrary to her early misgivings about Tasmania, Harriet came to love her new home and was genuinely grieved when Thomas was replaced by Charles Du Cane[40] and his wife Georgiana in December 1868. During her six years' residence in the colony, Harriet, through her travelling, tireless benevolent work (even while heavily pregnant), and multifarious vice-regal duties, had established strong connections with people from all walks of life, including princes and convicts, raised and co-educated six happy and healthy children and had alleviated the suffering of many people struggling in an economic depression.

Thirty years later, in November 1898, the 69-year-old widow, now known as Lady Gore Browne, (after Thomas' knighthood in 1869), revisited her beloved Tasmania[41] and was received enthusiastically by the ladies of Hobart (as it was now called). In her touching farewell speech, she declared that:

> I feared I should be like Rip Van Winkle, forgotten, and looking in vain for welcome recognition; but it is evident that "out of sight out of mind" is a proverb unknown in Tasmania.[42]

■ ■ ■

ENDNOTES

1. Sir Henry Edward Fox Young, Tasmanian Governor during the period 1855–1862. His wife was Lady Augusta Sophia Young, nee Marryat.
2. Archives New Zealand (hereafter ANZ), Diary of Harriet Louisa Gore Browne, December 5, 1861, ADCZ 17007, W5431/8.
3. ANZ, Diary of Harriet Louisa Gore Browne, September 9, 1860, ADCZ 17007, W5601/1.
4. James Campbell, lawyer and businessman.
5. A British territory in the South Atlantic Ocean, approximately 2,000 km west of the south-western coast of Africa.
6. ANZ, Diary of Harriet Louisa Browne, September 18, 1855, ADCZ 17007, W5601/1.
7. ANZ, Diary of Harriet Louisa Gore Browne, May 1856, ADCZ 17007, W5601/1 (p.63 on digitised copy, accessed through ARCHWAY website: https://www.archway.archives.govt.nz/FullItem.do)
8. Ibid.
9. ANZ, Diary of Harriet Louisa Browne, September 24, 1860, ADCZ 17007, W5601/1.
10. Jane Maria Atkinson, nee Richmond (1824–1904) was a British-born community leader in New Zealand.
11. Correspondence from Jane Maria Atkinson to Margaret Taylor, October 3, 1860, in A. H. McLintock (ed.), *The Richmond-Atkinson Papers*, Vol. 1 (Government Printer, Wellington, 1960), p.641.
12. Harriet Louisa Gore Browne, (W. P. Morrell ed.), *Narrative of the Waitara Purchase and the Taranaki War* (Dunedin, University of Otago Press, 1965).
13. Including Messrs Edward Stafford and Cracroft Wilson.
14. Mr Dick quote, mentioned in (ANZ), Diary of Harriet Louisa Gore Browne, June 15, 1861, ADCZ 17007, W5431/7.
15. Sir George Grey was an experienced but controversial Governor who had previously governed New Zealand from 1845–1853. At the time of his redeployment to New Zealand in late 1861, he was Governor at the Cape Colony (South Africa).
16. ANZ, Diary of Harriet Louisa Gore Browne, September 27, 1861, ADCZ 17007, W5431/7.
17. ANZ, Diary of Harriet Gore Browne, October 10, 1861, ADCZ 17007, W5431/7.
18. Harriet and Thomas stayed at Government House in Sydney with NSW Governor, Sir John Young and his wife Lady Adelaide Annabella Tuite Young, nee Dalton.
19. *Mercury*, December 11, 1861, p.2.
20. The budget allocated to the Governor's establishment was reduced from £2,500 to £1,000, ANZ, Diary of Harriet Louisa Gore Browne, November 2, 1862, ADCZ 17007, W5431/8.

21. ANZ, Diary of Harriet Louisa Gore Browne, January 24, 1862, ADCZ 17007, W5431/8.
22. Charlotte Macdonald, "Power that Hurts: Harriet Gore Browne and the perplexities of living inside empire", *Itinerario*, Vol. 42, No, 1, 24, 2018, Research Institute for History, Leiden University.
23. The Cascade Female Factory in Degraves Street, South Hobart. It was previously used to house only female convicts, but after convict transportation to Tasmania ended in 1853 it was proclaimed a gaol in 1856 (femalefactory.org.au/history/)
24. ANZ, Diary of Harriet Louisa Browne, January 24, 1862, ADCZ 17007, W5431/8.
25. ANZ, Diary of Harriet Louisa Gore Browne, January 10, 1862, ADCZ 17007, W5431/8.
26. ANZ, Diary of Harriet Louisa Browne, January 8, 1863, ADCZ 17007, W5431/8.
27. ANZ, Diary of Harriet Louisa Gore Browne, January 14, 1862, ADCZ 17007, W5431/8).
28. Ibid.
29. ANZ, Diary of Harriet Louisa Browne, December 29, 1861, ADCZ 17007, W5431/7.
30. Marion Boyd, incidentally, periodically lived as Harriet's companion at Government House.
31. ANZ, Diary of Harriet Louisa Gore Browne, April 23, 1862, ADCZ 17007, W5431/8.
32. ANZ, Diary of Harriet Louisa Browne, January 7, 1862, ADCZ 17007, W5431/8.
33. ANZ, Diary of Harriet Louisa Gore Browne, March 4, 1862, ADCZ 17007, W5431/8.
34. ANZ, Diary of Harriet Gore Browne, February 23, 1862, ADCZ 17007, W5431/8.
35. ANZ, Diary of Harriet Louisa Gore Browne, January 8, 1863, ADCZ 17007, W5431/8.
36. French Prince Pierre Philippe Jean Marie d'Orleans (1845–1919) was the exiled grandson of King Louis Philippe I.
37. The prince was accompanied by his relative, friend and biographer, Count Ludovic de Beauvoir and Albert-Auguste Fauvey. The visit to Hobart Town was part of a larger tour of Australia and parts of Asia and America, and in London 1870 de Beauvoir's travel journals were published in 2 volumes, entitled, *A Voyage around the World*.
38. Steve Harris, *The Prince and the Assassin: Australia's first Royal tour and portent of world terror* (Melbourne Books, Melbourne, Victoria, 2017).
39. ANZ, Diary of Harriet Louisa Gore Browne, January 19, 1868, ADCZ 17007, W5431/10.
40. Ibid.
41. ANZ, Diary of Harriet Louisa Gore Browne, March 9, 1868, ADCZ 17007, W5431/10.

42. Charles Du Cane (later "Sir"), British Conservative Party politician, colonial administrator and later the Governor of Tasmania (January 15, 1869–January 30, 1874). Du Cane was later knighted and became Sir Du Cane.
43. Harriet was accompanied by her youngest daughter, Mrs Ethel Locke King and her husband Hugh, Commander Godfrey Gore Browne (her youngest son) and Fred Steward who was Thomas' cousin and former Private Secretary. Their visit was part of a world tour.
44. *Mercury*, December 30, 1898, 3.

The forgotten birdsmith

ERICA NATHAN

If Michael Sharland could write from the grave his words would betray a whiff of injury:

> I am, or rather was, Peregrine, nature columnist of sixty years, beginning in 1921, mainly for the *Mercury* weekend edition that serviced southern Tasmania. Unless you are over fifty, you may not remember me, and sadly my public memorial is unlikely to jolt your memory. My name garnishes a forested knoll, one of the sugarloafs, on the edge of the island's central plateau. Like the ghost roads of old, "Sharland" exists more as cartographic fabrication. You'll find me on "Shannon", number 8213 in the 1:100,000 series.
>
> Birds were my big love. They flew into my time on the farm, along the coast, on bush excursions, and in the garden, and then there were moments when I followed them into terrain off grid and off the island. Hard-won photos always helped support the weekly column and I took that skill on as a young lad not far from here in Campbell Town.

I wish to speak for Sharland. Not because he was an especially gifted writer, or reached beyond the assumptions of his time – I am intrigued by his journalistic longevity, his populist readership across the island state of Tasmania, and the conservation community stimulated by his words. There is, in this turbulent, Covid-transformed era, great questing for the salve of the natural world, a need to share words of observation and experience, and yet, there is also disquiet about this particular literary genre. See, I also have qualms about using the term "nature writing", as have others, and there are good reasons.

Sharland had no such qualms. Although he began as a general news journalist, working in Melbourne and Sydney, he was to identify primarily as a nature writer. His stylistic roots were English, in a tradition excelling at a parish scale. For perhaps the first four decades Sharland's writing, supported by his photography, was not unusual. A nature column was a featured highlight of several national and regional newspapers across Australia. It is likely that the Melbourne-centred influence of journalist-writers Donald McDonald (*The Argus*) and then Charles Barrett (*The Herald*) extended across Bass Strait to reach a young Sharland. They were disciplined amateurs, out there at nature's coalface, spotting, discerning, photographing, writing, galvanising reader response. Most differentiated themselves happily from the later authority of the more aloof university professional.[1]

Indeed, there is tragedy and pathos in this telling. As the authority of environmental science began to nip at Sharland's amateur heels, he shared an increasing bitterness with fellow writer-naturalists who had also tramped and photographed to bodily limits at times. He fell, but did not plummet between the cliffs of gentleman amateur and environmental professional, and perhaps it was his loyal readership that saved him from the chasm. There was another cliff-face he was blind to, and of course, it would be difficult to write across six decades and remain present in each. As the 1960s rolled into the 1970s, and then 1980s, it became increasingly apparent that his narrative vignettes were often situated uncritically inside white settler stories, infused with an overdose of their rural nostalgia. He remained inside those stories.

For all that, I hear him from the grave, and his voice has value still.

Sharland was born on the very brink of the 20th century, in 1899, and his ornithological foothold was in both centuries. He spent most of his early years in Campbell Town and at a nearby smallholding to the east of the town, Kearney Bogs. Expressing his own nostalgia, he paid homage to his Midlands roots in *Wheelbarrow Fantasy*.[2] Sharland reminisced about his route into the world of nature, as a youngster, following the wheelbarrow tracks made by an elderly local who foraged the town perimeter for firewood. Tussock and sedge grassland created an exploratory otherworld all scaled to a bantam Sharland. He hesitated to enter the forest beyond, "being too dark and scary inside". By listening to his friend's bush escapades, full of wildlife trapping, he was prepped to hurdle the fenced threshold into the forests of his island home. Sharland reflected, "To the end of this old man's days, he probably wouldn't have known that his wheelbarrow tracks, formed from sweat and hard work, had once served me as a playground."

Sharland did not conclude with this reflection. As with many of his columns, there was carry over correspondence that generated webs of connection across the island. A Campbell Town relative identified Sharland's foraging friend as Alexander Wrankmore. Readers would learn that he helped to raise his widowed sister's large family in the two-roomed house near the tussocks, and that in his 90th year, Alexander died from injuries received in a small pen when butted by a ram. In this way Sharland's writing reverberated into far-flung pockets of settler experience. He regularly included narrative tangents that hooked contributions from his readers.

Sharland's participatory readers were from suburban backyards, the farms of the Midlands, the bush of the Central Highlands. His archived letters, as well as those reader fragments integrated into his column, show how values of wildlife conservation were transmitted in newsprint, enlivened by the reading, the responding, and the sharing.[3] Some readers carried their own nature-loving lore, such as the Wilson family of the Steppes, or, Deny King, from remote Melaleuca in the south-west wilderness. These special correspondents were nodes in a network that criss-crossed the island, giving authority to local landscapes seen, heard, and interrogated first hand. Sharland, always *Peregrine* to his readers, was a kind of curator in this process.

∎

During those years that Sharland created his tussocked realm, he was educated at the local grammar school and then at the government school. From Michael Roe's biographical sketch, it is also apparent that Sharland experienced a rather fragmented family life.[4] As a young man he joined his recently divorced mother in Hobart, where, after some faltering, he entered the world of newspapers as copy boy. The main body of his journalistic work was based in Tasmania, and about Tasmania. He did publish independently, most notably his *Stones of the Century*, in 1952, and he also had several "bird" titles relating to Tasmania and further afield. And he did have other roles, most notably as secretary of the Scenery Preservation Board, from 1947, for more than a decade. Financially, and professionally, this particular role was critical in supporting his newspaper column.

ERICA NATHAN The forgotten birdsmith

Sharland's sooty tern narrative composed for his personal album.
Tasmanian Archives (NS1179/2/3)

Sharland's life thread was his weekly nature column. Perhaps most evocative of the younger Sharland are his annotated photographic albums that lie patiently in the Tasmanian archives.[5] Every page is a thoughtful composition featuring silver scroll flourishes and descriptive captions, some waggish, that exult his photos of nests and birds, field excursions and campouts, coastal and bush scenes. In these albums you feel the intensity and excitement of his learning about the natural world. Sharland transitioned from displaying his own photographic exploits to publishing nature narratives in the local newspaper. He continued to organise his photos methodically around special excursions. Even the collation of his 1945 Mutton Bird album, with photos of birders enduring inspection, and mountains of lifeless birds at the cannery, retained a child-like quality.[6]

Photography did help Sharland establish a career path. The Museum of Applied Arts and Sciences holds some of his early camera equipment, and a few thousand of his negatives and prints are held by the Australian Museum.[7] He had other help. In the 1920s and 1930s, Sharland was not alone in climbing trees, constructing platforms, camouflaging cameras and stalking his subject.

Part record of Sharland's camping excursion at Mt Field, from his personal album.
Tasmanian Archives (NS1179/2/1)

There was a growing number of state and national nature organisations that supported his interest. Sharland was active in a field naturalists club from his early 20s, but when even younger than that he was part of club excursions. These albums, and his field journals, record the hijinks and collegiality that intertwined with his bird study.

These amateur groups with their field trips and journals and networks that extended across Australia and overseas, offered Sharland both an education and a model of knowledge underscored by ground-truthing, and a sharing ethos. It was the Royal Australian Ornithologists' Union (RAOU) that received most commitment from Sharland, even if this loyalty was sorely tested in later years. Historian Libby Robin argues that ornithology as a modern scientific discipline is distinguished and strengthened by its inclusive blurring of the professional and the amateur.[8] At the time Sharland was shaping his career this blurring was at its most inconclusive, and by the end of his working life he clearly felt on the margins of a world to which he had once been centrally connected through a network of field-based observers.

Hobart was home to some quite extraordinary ornithologists during Sharland's lifetime. Topping the list was Robert Hall, recently mentioned in Andrew Darby's *Flight Lines*, which follows the history of migratory bird science.[9] Sharland knew and respected this great globe wanderer who tracked birds on their migrations, taking their skins to piece together trajectories. Late in his career Hall came to Hobart and became a curator and director of the Tasmanian Museum and Art Gallery, but by the time he was a mentor figure for Sharland, his professional life had ended. Hall did attempt to instruct the novice bird enthusiast – in his early 20s at the time – in the art of skinning. The unsuccessful apprentice remembered the blood and feathers that filled Hall's kitchen.[10]

When Hall died in 1949, the cultural tide had turned against defending the collector tradition in the name of science. Although Sharland was part of introducing this change, he recognised the professional reach, and generosity of Robert Hall, successfully bidding for items of his estate, including several hundred skins and an expedition diary. He retained the diary, and in 1975 sold the collection of skins, and a nine-drawer cabinet, to the Melbourne Museum.

Colonel William Vincent Legge was another ornithological great living in Hobart. Like Hall, he was on the founding committee for RAOU (and its first president). They had both published serious reference books and contributed scholarly articles that informed the international debates of the new science. Sharland had access to this more academic literature in lieu of a more formal education in the sciences. Only 20 years old when Legge died, Sharland retained a selection of articles gifted to him by the son of a G. K. Hinsby, a well-known bird enthusiast and collector from Tasmania's west coast.[11] Both the papers and their provenance encapsulate the varied streams of Sharland's learning.

Sharland's Tasmanian excursions shifted to more extended trips across mainland Australia and later to overseas. On occasions, his long-time correspondent and lifelong friend, the respected amateur ornithologist Keith Hindwood, from Sydney, joined him. Alec Chisholm was another regular correspondent. Both published more widely than Sharland, but likewise shared generational challenges, tinged by the inherited traditions of Australian ornithology while at the same time responding to the demands of a readership in the second half of the 20th century. Through various projects and newsletters they constituted a semi-professional network.

For Sharland, birds were his nature touchstone. The essential thread of his columns was the interaction people had with birds, and more generally, with their natural environs. His subject was primarily "nature" as experienced by the curious, patient and local observer, a figure modelled on himself, and those like him. Week after week he exported the idea of shared nature knowing. Sharland wrote about the forty spotted pardalotes nesting at Tinderbox.[12] He corresponded with the local landholder. They surveyed the nests over several years, learning together, and this knowledge was recycled in his column. Sharland's field observations, from trips far and near, gave him a gumboot experience of the country that he believed the new scientists, with their tables and statistics, were lacking.[13] His readers, many in actual gumboots, likely felt the same.

Sharland's style of journalism celebrated the shared learning and enthusiasm of the natural history groups of which he was a member and, on occasions, was to lead. Generally he did not hitch his musings to nationalist ideals, preferring to stay anchored to his field-studying, camera-wielding self. His tone would be intimate as he shared jigsaw pieces of information. He often weaved "we" and "our" into his narrations. "Although we know the black cockatoo breeds in a hollow limb or a hollow in a tree … it occurred to us that these big birds, in the absence of suitable tree hollows might breed in the holes and crevices so numerous in the cliffs of this range."[14] He hypothesised about cockatoo nidification (a word borrowed from Sharland with thanks), and readers perceived knowledge in the making. Sharland's writing would bubble up from an observation or the kink in a story while his conservation principles, egg protection in this instance, rested just below the surface in a secondary contextual manner.

Sharland came at birds from many angles, with the following article headings just a sample:[15] Birds at Full Moon, Seabirds of Bruny Island, Thrushes in Snow, Swans by Night, Black and White Birds, Birds of the Buttongrass, Singers of the Sedges, A Bird that lines its Nest with Human Hair, Bird Migrants Return, An Extinct Bird, Why Does the Blue Wren Peck at Your Window? Lyrebird Arguments, Curious Habits of the Cuckoo, "First Swallow" May Never Have Been Away, Ducks are Cunning, Birds seek Company, Birdland Oddities.

Sharland wanted readers of his more than 3,000 articles to *like* birds. Implicit in his writing was that a collective fondness for the avian species enabled localised nature to be explored and scrutinised, to be experienced through protective, nurturing and collaborative knowing. This primary tack did not preclude him from a more overt conservation stance when outside the bounds of his column.[16] He defended the integrity of Port Arthur, Hobart's waterfront, Lake Pedder and national parks. Politically, within organisations, he protested unnecessary tree clearance and heritage vandalism. And indeed, much of his writing, published and in manuscript, has potential to benchmark the island of Tasmania as a changing natural domain. Sharland's regular observations of his favourite haunts, such as Rokeby Beach, Carlton River, Lake Tiberias and Moulting Lagoon, highlight the now and then potential of his articles.

It is often revealing those keepsakes that survive the downsizing of lives to find archival care. Sharland held on to items belonging to his maternal grandfather, the respected explorer-surveyor-politician, James Reid Scott.[17] It is unclear how and when Michael received his grandfather's records, or whether they played a major role in sparking his particular interest in birds. During the 1860s, Scott assembled a collection of birds' eggs in a box of Huon pine. He appended a folio of earnest drawings for the 50-odd eggs; a sketch plan of the box layout, as well as descriptive notes from Gould's *The Birds of Australia* (1848). This colonial cache was intended for a cousin returning to England, but at some point fell into the hands of Sharland, born 12 years after the early death of his grandfather.

It is likely that Sharland was ambivalent about this oological inheritance. Early on in his career Sharland joined those naturalists critical of the collector fetish that sanctioned shooting, preserving, and pilfering. On the other hand, he was proud to claim links to one of the elite families of white settler Tasmania. I like to imagine a young Sharland poring over the pencil sketches of his grandfather, who was careful to identify the different shell markings at the "large end and the small end" of his eggs. Many of Sharland's photographs featured eggs in the nest, and the decorated albums are testament to Sharland's learning about his local birds as he also surveyed the island. In the same way James Reid Scott coveted his egg collection, arranging them just so, Sharland found a visceral connection with birds through his photographic compositions.

Sharland's weekend columns were published as *Tracks of the Morning*, to commemorate his unbroken 60-year penmanship. This followed on from his 50-year commemorative edition, *A Pocketful of Nature*. The earlier dust jacket of a trekking bush camper, axe in hand, gave way to the more acceptable 1970s image of Sharland strolling through foothill forest, along an established trail, binoculars at the ready.

Tracks of the Morning cover showing Michael Sharland.
Courtesy of the Mercury, *Hobart*

Sharland, and his publishers, did try to fine-tune him to changing times. Inevitably Sharland's relevance waned as the world he knew in his prime altered. By the time he died, just a few years after retiring as *Peregrine*, he was barely honoured for his six decades of bird-smithing.

■

For much of the 20th century, Sharland was known as *the* nature writer for the island of Tasmania. This appellation clouds his legacy, for the idea of "nature writing" is tethered to a white colonial tradition, and to a worldview that places people as subjects acting in and on an objectified space called nature. Sharland's stupendous output was instrumental in nurturing, with apparent innocence, Tasmania as knowable, rich in a new nomenclature for bush and birds that erased the indigenous world. His was nature for white settlers and their descendants, a step beyond the threatening wildness of early contact colonisation, and an unimaginable leap from indigenous knowing.

In Australia, how to write about nature is contentious, but the practice is evolving with greater consciousness of the chemistry between a deep past and a present in motion. In Tasmania, lutruwita continues to break through. Sharland would not survive scrutiny today, and yet, there are seams of his writing that have an insistent attraction, and validity. For six decades, Sharland's writing did ignite warmth, sharing, respect and curiosity across a popular, if incomplete, island readership. How he achieved this is worth remembering. What he observed and recorded is deserving of our attention.

Vale Sharland.

■ ■ ■

ENDNOTES

1. Tom Griffiths, *Hunters and Collectors: The Antiquarian Imagination in Australia* (Cambridge; Melbourne: Cambridge University Press: 1996), 121–149.
2. Michael Sharland, *Tracks of the Morning* (Hobart: The Mercury Newspaper, 1981), 1–5.
3. Tasmanian Archives: Michael Sharland and Family NS 1179/1/1-3, 1/2 May 1920, Deny King; 1/3 Madge Wilson.
4. Michael Roe, "Michael Sharland: For Nature and Heritage", *Tasmanian Historical Research Association, Papers and Proceedings* 55, No.1 (2008): 44–63.
5. Tasmanian Archives: Michael Sharland and Family NS 1179, In particular 1/50; 1/51; 1/55; 2/1; 2/2; The Mutton Bird: 1/52.
6. Tasmanian Archives NS1179/1/52.
7. Australian Museum Archives: series 268 for his photographs. More relevant for this essay is the holding of Sharland's field notebooks and diaries: Papers of M. R. S. Sharland AMS 191, 1918–1981. A small selection is available online.
8. Libby Robin, *The Flight of the Emu: A hundred years of Australian ornithology 1901–2001* (Carlton, Vic.: Melbourne University Press: 2001), chapter 7.
9. Andrew Darby, *Flight Lines: Across the globe on a journey with the astonishing ultramarathon birds* (Crows Nest, NSW: Allen & Unwin: 2020), 133–4.
10. Michael Sharland, Obituary Robert Hall, *The Emu* 49, No.49 (1949): 144-5; Tasmanian Archives: NS1179/1/2 His notes for an article about Hall. 11.
11. Tasmanian Archives: NS1179/1/42.

12. AMS: 191 Field Note Book No. 17: 30, 32–3.
13. For example, Tasmanian Archives: NS1179/1/2 Letter to book editor April 18, 1977.
14. Michael Sharland, *A Pocketful of Nature* (Hobart: The Mercury Newspaper, 1971), 29–30.
15. Tasmanian Archives: NS1179/36 Bound volume of press cuttings.
16. For Sharland's valuing of built heritage see Stefan Petrow,"Conservative and reverent souls: the growth of historical consciousness in Tasmania 1935–60", Public History Review, Vol. 11 (2004): 149–50 and Michael Roe (2008). He was on a number of conservation committees and his support for particular issues is evident in the Tasmanian Archives NS1179 correspondence files.
17. Tasmanian Archives NS1179/34.

The eternal return of Tasmanian trauma

ROHAN PRICE

I have a confession to make. My family benefited from violent clearance of the Tasmanian Aborigines (or Palawa) from a quarter of Van Diemen's Land by its most prominent land company. One reckoning put the total number of Aborigines around Circular Head in the far north-west of the colony in the early 1820s at around 500 souls; a year after the arrival of the Van Diemen's Land Company (VDL Company) in 1826 that number had fallen to a mere 100 or so due in significant part to a sustained campaign of violence overseen by the Company's chief agent, Edward Curr (1798–1850).[1] The trauma caused by this annihilation flares up to this day in disagreements about preservation of Aboriginal heritage on the northwest and west coasts. Palawa ancestral suffering is likely to continue as an infinite loop until the chain of opportunity enjoyed by VDL Company descendants can be spoken about openly.

A few days shy of her eightieth birthday, my mother, who came from Burnie, acknowledged to me that my grandfather two generations back, James Norton Smith, had been chief agent and manager of the VDL Company. I looked into this. Indeed, Curr had been the first chief agent, then James Gibson, then Charles Nichols and old James Snr became general manager in 1869. After an indifferent period for the company under Nichols, Norton Smith had taken the helm and apparently restored the company's fortunes. He moved its headquarters from Launceston to Emu Bay (Burnie), established a Hereford cattle stud at the company's show-property Woolnorth and a railway to transport Mount Bischoff tin deposits to Emu Bay in the 1870s and 1880s.[2]

He finally retired in 1903.³ In revealing these things, I understood why my own grandfather, also named James Norton Smith, spent his life as a locomotive engineer on the Zeehan-Emu Bay railway line and why my older brother's middle name is James.

The VDL Company had been given by the colonial government unchallengeable rights of land selection from Cape Grim to Fort Sorrell (now Port Sorrell, about 20 kilometres east of Devonport). Wherever the Company selected land, the Aborigines were exiled, shot or pushed-off. Curr became notorious for covering up a massacre of up to 30 local male Aborigines on VDL Company lands at Cape Grim on 10 February 1828.⁴ Relying on three separate sources, Lyndall Ryan confirmed an account that four shepherds had "crept up" on Aborigines while they were hunting and "shot 30 dead and threw their bodies to the rocks below".⁵ Female Aboriginal witnesses who subsequently gave evidence were adamant that "many" women were killed.⁶

On the events of February 10, 1828 Edward Curr initially maintained that there had been six victims at Cape Grim, later changed it to only three, and that he had, as de facto magistrate in the area, decided that any liability detected by an enquiry "would induce every man to leave the Cape".⁷ The massacre was left unreported to Lieutenant Governor Arthur for two years, it has been speculated that Curr "believed the violence against the Aborigines at Cape Grim constituted legitimate defence of company property, but lacked the confidence to test this theory by informing the lieutenant governor".⁸ G. A. Robinson, who reported to the lieutenant governor, and led the eventual inquiry into the massacre, knew that Curr was implicated in many Palawa shooting deaths.⁹ It is likely that Curr refrained from telling Arthur about the second Cape Grim massacre, at least in part, because his wide freedom of action under the colonial government could be decreased by full disclosure. In the previous month, he had played down the report that 12 Aborigines had been killed by four shepherds at Cape Grim who had retreated to a VDL Company ship by saying their guns "misfired" and nobody was killed.¹⁰

In the final year of the Black War in April 1831, Edward Curr observed a group of 12 Aborigines at Mount Cameron who would not come down from the hills when he beckoned them.¹¹ He supposed a détente in their relations had arisen because his party was unarmed at the time and the Aborigines "could easily have injured us if they wished but they made no attempt to molest us".¹² In June 1832, Curr became confident that there would be no more Aborigines on Company land. Curr reported: "I trust & believe that I shall have no more reports to make of our people being murdered by the natives ... I am satisfied we have seen the end."[13] What he really wanted to convey to his company masters in London was that there were no more unpacified Aborigines living in tribal groups on the northwest coast of Tasmania by that time because he had taken care of the problem.

The decline of the Palawa population across the colony had been swift. It has been estimated that there were between 4,000 and 9,000 Palawa in 1803 and about 200 remained by 1835.[14] Curr noted that 80 Aborigines had been taken to the settlement at Wybalenna by G.A. Robinson in June 1832. Using his broad brush, Curr contended that these people constituted "all the tribes which have infested the settled districts and committed so many murders".[15] He was correct that failed the Black Line in 1830 had expelled the Aborigines to the coastal fringes; his blanket assumption of their homicidal guilt created a narrative of them getting what they deserved.

Curr mentioned in his correspondence in December 1832 that Anthony Cottrell, who was a deputy of G. A. Robinson's Friendly Mission, had "encountered forty adults on the West Coast South of the Arthur River".[16] Cottrell had only lured away seven of them; "the others shewing a determined spirit of hostility".[17] Not only had the remnant members of the North-Western Tribe retreated to the district containing their sacred petroglyphs, and resisted Cottrell's cossetting advances, they told him, in the spirit of leading him a merry dance, that they were heading for the (Hampshire) Hills – something that he did not believe.[18] The 12 Aborigines that Curr had failed to bring down the hill east of Woolnorth at Mount Cameron in April 1831 had also retreated into the sacred, as there are large, well-documented petroglyphs there, too.[19] This area became the Preminghana Indigenous Protected Area in 1999.

The VDL Company's legacy is marked by the Palawa trauma its employees instigated at Woolnorth and elsewhere. Psychoanalyst Robert Stolorow contended that colonial trauma victims and their ancestors live a "dark foreboding ... of traumatic temporality".[20] They "bear the agony" of "the eternal return of the same".[21] Tasmanian life has quietly found expression in this portal of Nietzschean thought. A dispute has been running since the late 1990s over the rare and eroding Palawa petroglyphs (stone carvings) eight kilometres south of the Arthur River on the West Coast[22] – where the sighting of the 40 adults had been made by Cottrell. Much of the problem concerning the preservation of the site lays in the Circular Head Aboriginal community not being recognised by the Tasmanian government as having any particular connection with the area or its carvings.²³ This dispute not only concerns who the Aborigines of the northwest coast are and why their ancestral claims have been rejected. Tasmania's old settler families provoke recurring trauma by maintaining an uneasy silence over commemoration of the atrocities and recognition of sacred areas. Edward Curr and the shepherds of the Van Diemen's Land Company were in the front line of the colonial atrocities.

I received the same information about the Palawa that most children growing up in Tasmania did. No-one could be unaware of Tasmanian Aboriginal leader Michael Mansell. He went on the news in the 1980s to publicise his trip to Libya in support of Aboriginal sovereignty, many prominent non-Indigenous Tasmanians stepped forward to vilify him.²⁴ At the time, Mansell seemed to me to be surrounded by controversy; he made waves. Grown-ups, it seemed, repudiated him for no clear reason. I suspect these days that some sort of displacement of object had occurred. Mocking him aided their "unconscious wish" not to be brought back to the site of atrocity.²⁵

Like many children the 1980s, I received an arbitrary education about the Palawa. We were left to draw a conclusion when told that they had no fish hooks, no barbs on their spear tips and only had fire from lightning strikes. The failure of the Black Line was taught as if proof that they were shifty as well as backward. Out of school, I heard stories that European property owners simply ran – at carbine point – tribes of Aborigines off a cliff to fall on to the stony coast below. Nobody came for the bodies because they jumped in family groups. They were left down there waiting overnight, some still groaning, for the great tidal surge of Bass Strait to claim them. Although the tales circulated as rural myths, ancestors of the white settlers knew better than to deny their truth.

Curr's cover-ups form almost no part of his legacy. He is remembered for his influence on the focus of Tasmanian history for a century after his time. He besmirched the Palawa as nothing more or less than a murderous menace. This became absorbed into the popular telling of history:

> And in the bush around the little settlement lurked the natives of the Emu Bay and Cape Grim mobs; wild, native, black savages fantastically daubed with red ochre, who speared the company's cattle and horses and took an occasional shot with their spears at one of the company's servants if they found him alone.²⁶

Offering warped readings of the past can cause fresh trauma. Jennifer Griffiths distinguished between the trauma of an event that "produces symptoms and calls for testimony" and, secondly, "socially produced trauma" that emanates from indifference to suffering in society and "failed witness".[27] One example of failed witness that comes to mind was the Curr-inspired denial of the events at the Cape Grim February massacre in a 1953 local history of Circular Head. It referred only to the burning by Aborigines of the shepherds' huts and their driving "a hundred valuable imported Merino ewes" over a 300 feet bank; this was reported to have occurred at "Slaughter Hill" near Cape Grim and "the few sheep that survived drowning they speared".[28] No mention was given of any Aboriginal deaths or any guess of a motive for them attacking the huts, if they did. This was more than indifference to the deaths of the Palawa. In history as life, they were cancelled out by a desire to tell a grand pastoral story.

My Mother was surprised when I told her that hundreds of Aboriginal people were killed in the forty years before old James Snr's time at the Company. Surprise might be understandable given the blanketing effect of denial but it is not helpful. Most of the old Tasmanian families, including mine, have consumed the fruits of the Palawa violence in one way or another. The issue these days is what we do about what we know. Our prosperity came from somewhere. It came at someone else's expense. Although "guilt" for my family's prosperity does not feel like the right word, no-one should knock at the veneers of inheritance expecting to hear a solid sound.

Nietzsche declared: "Life itself is *essentially* appropriation, injury, overpowering ... the weaker, suppression, severity ..."[29] If there was only violent appropriation in a will to power, then nothing humane or consoling can come out of recalling atrocity. If we are tempted to be triumphal about the the houses, the fencing, the railways and ports, then no repentance or request for forgiveness can be real. Burying the past becomes a step on the road to greatness. Trauma contests this. It produces a never-ending series of questions for survivor and perpetrator. Guilt is weakness in Nietzsche's great game of dog-eat-dog. Yet trauma has a long memory.

Most people in the personalised history game are looking for an agreeable fiction, not trauma or responsibility for its reverberations. My quest to know could be seen as perverse. But it is pathological to leave history as a cultivated ignorance. The endlessly interwoven destinies and the fictions that brought comfort to wrongdoers on a small island like Tasmania are easy to find if you are looking. In my mind's eye, I want to scissor out the human figures of the famous conciliatory poster of 1828, "Governor Arthur's Proclamation to the Aborigines".[30] I want to rearrange them – a white woman with an Aboriginal baby, an Aboriginal woman with a white baby, the Aborigine hung for a white murder, the white hung for an Aboriginal murder – underneath the tines of a descendancy chart. I will call my pastiche, "Who Do You Think You Were?"

There is no walking back from the rule of abusive instinct in early colonial times. For some settlers, the shooting of pheasants, hares and quail introduced from England was barely distinguished from stalking fellow humans. William Knight, a settler implicated in the shooting of dozens of Aborigines in the Meander River region in June 1827 was reported by a stockkeeper to "kill Aborigines for sport".[31] The chill of this comment reminded me of a reprisal raid by a group of mainland Native Troopers let loose in 1853 on a remnant population of Aborigines around Port Curtis (Gladstone, Queensland) "for a month of sharp shooting".[32] In another Tasmanian account, it was said "privately" that "up country" [north central midlands and Meander] "instances occur where the Natives are shot like so many crows".[33]

The repetitious loop of violence comes around again and again in ancestral echoes. Palawa descendants are derided as having no stake in history or current policy. The Circular Head Aboriginal community, for example, has been outraged that the government of Tasmania wants to reopen four wheel drive tracks in the Tarkine region, and that whilst it has been closed, quadbikes have driven over ancient middens at Interview River.[34] One wants to believe such acts are those of the ignorant. Thoughtless acts nevertheless reinjure the traumatised. Learning that purposeful denigration of a site had occurred could only hurt more.

The potted history of the Circular Head region written by a local hand in 1953 could never include a balanced treatment of the Cape Grim massacre or its reverberations in the trauma experienced today. It does, however, demonstrate how narrow the concerns of any history can be. The silence of those who hold knowledge of atrocity is a re-traumatising act waiting to happen. Acknowledging, at the very least, trauma as an explanation for the discord that exists now, and presuming heavily the recurrence of trauma in post-colonial encounters, seems like a reasonable place to make a start.

As recently as 1934 there were tributes to Edward Curr from adventure writer Thomas Dunbabin. Curr was "a man of learning and piety", "a kind-hearted man" and one "who did what he could for the comfort and instruction of the motley band who served the company at this remote post".[35] A conclusion drawn from Griffiths could be that when debilitation of a victim is triggered by people who refuse to speak up about an old trauma, such complicity *should* amount to guilt, not solely in a phenomenological contention, but in the serious frown of law, too.[36] Chances for repenting need to be limited when opportunities for it have been ignored.

What can anyone from the old families do about the troubled history? Strategic silence and the realm of false beatification needs calling out. Do not continue to believe a stereotype or received wisdom after it has been refuted is also sound advice. Follow up a strong rumour or a footnote alike. Test the denial of violence. Be open to the story of Tunnerminnerwait, a Parperloihener man who was born on Robbins Island; as an eleven year old, he saw most of his family shot to death at the Cape Grim massacre.[37]

"The deaths and desecration of the Palawa [and] the defilement of Palawa bodies" suggested Nicholas Smith "form a profound disturbance in the Australia psyche".[38] Remembrance of Tasmania's one-time Premier, William Crowther (1817–1885) has been a recent example of the eternal return. He stood as an intelligent man, who, as a doctor, concerned himself with the alleviation of suffering. Yet despite his enlightenment, he grafted the deciduous cuttings of anthropological attitude to a branch of false reason. Ultimately weighting policy by race made him an effective colonial performer in an age when radical ideas of racial equality existed only in a reclusive constitution and a pious suggestion about all of us being God's children. As a matter of policy, equality before the law was not openly refuted or accepted by the colonial state in the last quarter of the nineteenth century. Keeping it in a grey zone allowed Crowther to dig up William Lanne's grave, remove his head and send it to London as if it was a paperweight.

Like Curr, Crowther situated the local Aborigines as "implacable enemies of the white race"[39] who after 1803 made conflict "to be the rule" and "to this mentality the Tasmanians [i.e. the Palawa] contributed".[40] The problem with this account? Even Palawa passivity was no path to salvation in colonial Tasmania. They were shot at like crows and forcibly evicted from their lands for sheep. In the colonial imaginary, their trauma did not need to be expiated. Had the Palawa been given human proximity, their thoughts, hopes and feelings, including their sense of loss, would have to be acknowledged. White ancestors should see the massacre acts infringing their humanity and finally see a shadow or two creeping over pioneer lives.

Denial of suffering back then, as now, loops into conversations about Tasmania's darkly magisterial past, the truth about its Renaissance Premier, its petroglyphs and wilderness tracks, putting barriers between Indigenous and non-Indigenous people that neither can "get over". We can begin again by naming the problem honestly. Michael Mansell does not want to make Tasmanians feel guilty about the sins of the past but for our state, our country to "wind back its domination, where domination is neither necessary nor justified."[41] A clearer picture of the colony waits for it too.

■ ■ ■

ENDNOTES

1. Geoff Lennox, "The Van Diemen's Land Company and the Tasmanian Aborigines: A Reappraisal" *Papers and Proceedings: Tasmanian Historical Research Association* 37 No. 4 (2010): 171.
2. Ekarestini O'Brien, *Australian Joint Copying Project Handbook Part 8 Miscellaneous Series* (3rd ed.) (Canberra: National Library of Australia, 1998) Entry 472, 184.
3. One reference in Peter Mercer, *Gateway to Progress: Centenary History of the Marine Board of Burnie* (Hobart: Marine Board of Burnie, 1969) 77 has James Norton Smith in this role in 1889–1898, and somewhat troublingly as the Master Warden of the Port of Burnie during 1889–1890 at the same time.
4. Nicholas Clements, *The Black War* (Brisbane: UQP, 2014) 181–2.
5. Lyndall Ryan, "Abduction and Multiple Killings of Aborigines in Tasmania" undated http://nationalunitygovernment.org/pdf/Aborigines_in_Tasmania.pdf, 17.
6. Ryan, "Abduction and Multiple Killings", 17.
7. Ian Macfarlane, *Beyond Awakening* (Launceston: Fullers, 2008) 123.
8. Samuel Furphy, *Edward M. Curr and the Tide of History* (Canberra: ANU E-Press, 2013) 11.
9. Norman Plomley (ed), *Friendly Mission: The Tasmanian Journals and Papers of George Augustus Robinson 1829–1834* (Kingsgrove, NSW: Halstead Press, 1966) 181–3, 192, 196–7, 202, 210, 231, 235, 603, 607, 689. Cited in Smith, *The Return of the Living Dead*, 282.
10. Ryan, "Abduction and Multiple Killings", 17.
11. J. M. Bruce (ed), *Van Diemen's Land Company: Letters, Dispatches, Minutes, Reports (1829–1847)* VDL 5/4 LHC VDLC Microfilm 34 Dispatch No. 173 (April 22, 1831).
12. Bruce, *Van Diemen's Land Company*, Dispatch No. 173 (April 22, 1831).
13. Bruce, *Van Diemen's Land Company*, VDL 5/4 HRL LHC VDLC Microfilm 34 – "Edward Curr to VDLC London" Dispatch No 218 (June 19, 1832).
14. Ryan, "Abduction and Multiple Killings", 15.
15. Bruce, *Van Diemen's Land Company*, Dispatch No. 218 (June 19, 1832).
16. Bruce, *Van Diemen's Land Company*, Dispatch No. 235 (December 7, 1832).

17. Bruce, *Van Diemen's Land Company*, Dispatch No. 235 (December 7, 1832).
18. Bruce, *Van Diemen's Land Company*, Dispatch No. 235 (December 7, 1832).
19. Tasmanian Archive, AA577/1/156, "Petroglyphs, Mt Cameron" General Correspondence – Lands and Surveys Department (1964–1965).
20. Robert Storolow "Portkeys, Eternal Recurrence and the Phenomenology of Traumatic Temporality", *International Journal of Psychoanalytic Self Psychology* 6 (2011): 436.
21. Storolow, "Portkeys, Eternal Recurrence", 436.
22. Hilary Burden, "Following in the Footsteps of Our People", *Tasmanian Times*, February 7, 2016, https://tasmaniantimes.com/2016/02/following-in-the-footsteps-of-our-first-people/.
23. Burden, "Following in the Footsteps".
24. Stan Grant, "An Indigenous Seventh State: A radical idea from a constitutional conservative" The Link Blog June 3, 2017 https://www.abc.net.au/news/2017-06-03/an-indigenous-seventh-state-radical-and-constitutional/8585078.
25. Gerald Izenberg, *The Existentialist Critique of Freud: The Crisis of Autonomy* (Princeton: Princeton University Press, 1976) 202.
26. Thomas Dunbabin, "Jorgen's Dogfish" *Sydney Daily Telegraph* reprinted in *The Advocate*, January 4, 1934, 6.
27. Jennifer Griffiths, "Between Women: Trauma, Witnessing and the Legacy of Interracial Rape in Robbie MacCaulay's Sally's Rape?", *Frontiers* 26 No. 3 (2005): 2.
28. K. R. Von Steiglitz, *A Short History of Circular Head and its Pioneers* (Launceston, 1952) 26.
29. Friedrich Nietzsche, *Beyond Good and Evil*, trans. R. J. Hollingdale (London: Penguin, 2009) 194. Emphasis in the original.
30. Rachel Franks, "Governor Arthur's Proclamation to the Aborigines" State Library of New South Wales blog, undated, https://www.sl.nsw.gov.au/stories/governor-arthurs-proclamation-aborigines.
31. Ryan, "Abduction and Multiple Killings", 15.
32. "Sydney News", *The Maitland Mercury and Hunter River General Advertiser*, June 15, 1853, 4.
33. Ryan, "Abduction and Multiple Killings", 24.
34. Lachlan Bennett, "Fresh Reports of Illegal Off-road Driving in the Tarkine ", *The Advocate*, April 6, 2018, https://www.theadvocate.com.au/story/5326954/fresh-reports-of-illegal-driving-in-the-tarkine/.
35. Dunbabin, "Jorgen's Dogfish", 6.
36. Griffiths, "Between Women: Trauma, Witnessing …", 3.
37. Lorena Allum, "The Forgotten War That Led to Port Phillip's First Public Executions" Radio National blog November 28, 2014 https://www.abc.net.au/radionational/programs/archived/hindsight/a-forgotten-war/5926302.
38. Nicholas Smith, "The Return of the Living Dead: Unsettlement and the Tasmanian tiger", *Journal of Australian Studies* 36 No. 3 (2012): 284
39. Crowther, "The Passing", 7.
40. Crowther, "The Passing", 6.
41. Grant, "An Indigenous Seventh State".

"Fiendish fondness for sin": homosexuality and the Tasmanian Gothic

In Tasmania, an empty wilderness was created, not found – a dark, unknown land where the wind whispers secrets too frightening to hear.[1]

DANIELLE SCRIMSHAW

On the pavement at Salamanca Place, Hobart, lies an inscription that lights up at night and reads "Forgive me for not holding you in my arms". The line reminds me of the title of Timothy Conigrave's memoir, *Holding The Man* (1995), a book I have read almost every year since discovering my bisexuality. There is a second sentence in the Salamanca pavement, which reads, "In the wake of your courage I swim", and together the sentences form Justy Phillips' installation *The Yellow Line*.

The art work was commissioned by the Hobart City Council and now serves as a permanent reminder of the 1988 Salamanca Market protests, an event which resulted in 130 arrests. Protesters were fighting against the council's ban on the stall of the Tasmanian Gay Law Reform Group (TGLRG) following a complaint which claimed the presence of openly gay and lesbian individuals was inappropriate at a family weekend market.[2] It was not so much queer representation specifically at Salamanca that was being fought for, but the right for queer and trans people to occupy any space within the state of Tasmania without being legally and socially required to hide their identity. Twenty-two years after South Australia became the first state to decriminalise male homosexuality in Australia, the Tasmanian Government ultimately yielded to legal pressures and followed suit in 1997.

A year following the Salamanca protest, an article discussing Tasmania's gothic nature by Jim Davidson was published in the literary journal *Meanjin*. Referring to the island state's geographical isolation, violent history and awe-inspiring landscape, Davidson discusses a variety of texts that evoke and emphasise the aesthetic of Tasmanian gothic. Queer literary theorists, such as Pauline Palmer, have recently analysed how queerness fits seamlessly into gothic narratives – the gothic genre itself is, arguably, intrinsically queer through its focus on the "uncanny". By transcending gender and sexual binaries, queer and trans people challenge heteronormative conventions in ways which produce fear, stigmatisation and discrimination. "Although lesbian and male gay sexuality is generally invisible," explains Palmer, "this, instead of necessarily protecting the queer individual, can exacerbate the hostility that his sexuality provokes if discovered."[3]

By considering the genre of Tasmanian Gothic in relation to the state's queer history, we can acknowledge how members of Tasmania's LGBTQI community have historically been othered in the past two centuries. When Australia was colonised by the British in 1788, laws which criminalised male homosexuality were introduced to the country and maintained until the late 20th century. Governor Arthur Phillip, of the First Fleet, infamously named murder and sodomy as the two crimes that would be punished by confining the offender "until an opportunity offered of delivering him to the natives of New Zealand, and let them eat him".[4] Although this never eventuated (most likely out of impracticality, more than anything), throughout global history homosexuality has consistently been considered disgusting and unnatural, almost monstrous. Portrayed by homophobic colonialists and more recent anti-gay groups as "evil", "fiendish" and "sinful", queer and trans individuals are central to Tasmania's gothic history.

TASMANIAN GOTHIC

Like Tasmania's campaign for gay law reform, the origins of the state's dark aesthetic came to life in the 1980s. Jim Davidson brought a name to this place-specific genre in his 1989 article *Tasmanian Gothic,* asserting that the island state was a landscape containing "absences" – "the slaughtered Aborigines, the downtrodden convicts, and hunted species like the diminutive Tasmanian Emu and the gothically named Tasmanian Tiger".[5]

A descendant of north-east Tasmania's Trawulwuy people, Greg Lehman, echoes this image of absence through his haunting remembrance, "I have found sadness in lonely places that were emptied of the living."[6] Tasmania's gothic narrative has additionally been established through Marcus Clarke's 1874 novel *For The Term of His Natural Life,* which was adapted into a televised mini-series in 1983, and Robert Hughes' convict history *The Fatal Shore*, released in 1987. Many films, novels, visual art, and even cultural festivals have continued to draw upon the Tasmanian gothic, finding inspiration in stories of the past, and a natural landscape that cannot be replicated anywhere else in Australia.

"I won't say it's always spooky," writes film-maker Briony Kidd, "but Tasmania does have a unique atmosphere, born of an unusually temperate climate for Australia, geographical isolation and memories of a violent past."[7]

Most scholarship on Tasmania's violent past has, understandably, focused on racial conflict such as the 19th-century's Black War, and the notoriety of Van Diemen's Land's convict prisons. Indigenous and convict narratives have regularly featured in the Tasmanian gothic, although the aesthetic, informed by a European sensibility, is not necessarily central to indigenous Tasmanian or non-European immigrant perspectives.[8]

In saying that, feelings of displacement and otherness carry layered meaning for queer people of colour. In addition to facing homophobia, racism has always been present since the colonisation of Australia, and racist attitudes are reflected by queer men and women as well as white heterosexuals. A member of the Gays and Lesbians Aboriginal Alliance recalled the discovery of his sexuality in the 1970s, saying, "It soon became apparent that, while some white guys would not hesitate to fuck with you, that didn't mean they had to say g'day to you in the street – which is exactly how most of them acted."[9] Narratives that evoke gothic elements of isolation, violence, and groups of people deemed different to the hegemonic mainstream, come in a variety of forms in the (queer) Tasmanian gothic.

Literary scholar Terry Castle utilises ghosts as a metaphor to discuss lesbianism in her book *The Apparitional Lesbian: Female Homosexuality and Modern Culture* (1993), claiming that queer women were never in the mainstream, but "in the shadows ... a wanderer in the dusk, a lost soul, a tragic mistake, a pale denizen of the night".[10] In other words, lesbians were treated in history, society and cultural narratives as though they were ghosts.

Considering that female homosexuality was not criminalised in Britain or Australia, only because heterosexual men could not comprehend the idea of women desiring sex and seeking physical and romantic attachments with other women, Castle's gothic metaphor is not an exaggeration. Rather than be discriminated against by the legal system, non-heterosexual women were simply not considered – they did not exist in the eyes of the law. But, as lesbian historian Martha Vicinus notes, queer women cannot simply be forgotten and so "she repeatedly reappears, haunting the heterosexual imaginary".[11]

Women may not have been arrested for homosexual acts, but they faced as much loathing and revulsion from society as gay men, with the addition of intense misogyny during the early colonial period. In Van Diemen's Land, there are several accounts of lesbian relationships between convicts in the Launceston, Ross and Hobart female factories.[12] Public outcry and fearmongering were regularly seen in the colonial press.

In March, 1840, the Hobart *Colonial Times* reported on a "flash mob" that was alleged to have been composed of a group of women who tormented and "seduced" other prisoners in the Female House of Correction. The anonymous author likens the flash mob to Johann Wolfgang von Goethe's tragic play *Faust*, emphasising certain gothic and sexual elements by drawing attention to the group's actions being "performed in the dark and silent hour of night ... in solitude and secrecy, amongst only the duly initiated".[13]

The author of this article writes in an exaggerated manner to win an effect on his readers, hoping to shock the free public of the colony by drawing on their fear and disgust. "With the fiendish fondness for sin," he continues, "every effort ... is made by these wretches to acquire proselytes to their infamous practices."[14] While the author is not specific about the women's "infamous practices" performed at night, it is heavily implied to be sexual. What's interesting with this article is the specific portrayal of queer convict women – not only are they already abhorred due to their convict status, their homosexuality degrades them as less than human. Lesbian convicts are likened to Goethe's "supernatural inhabitants", emphasising their unnaturalness and bringing these women firmly into Tasmania's gothic potential.

SALAMANCA MARKET, 1988

Decriminalisation of male homosexuality began with the gay rights movement in the 1970s, with the majority of mainland states and territories having removed discriminatory laws by the end of the 1980s. The campaign within Tasmania required outside intervention, from the United Nations Human Rights Committee and the Federal Government, which passed an anti-discriminatory law in 1994 that legalised sexual activity between consenting adults throughout Australia.[15] As a result of Tasmanian law conflicting with the Commonwealth, TGLRG members Rodney Croome and Nicholas Toonen lodged a statement with the High Court of Australia in 1995 to declare certain sections of the Tasmanian Criminal Code as invalid.[16] The case continued for almost two years until male homosexuality was decriminalised by the Tasmanian Government in 1997. Member of Legislative Council George Brookes described the occasion as "a very sad day for Tasmania".[17]

The campaign for gay law reform in Tasmania is often considered to have begun in 1988, when the Tasmanian Gay Law Reform Group began setting up a stall at the Salamanca Market, distributing leaflets and collecting signatures for petitions. The Hobart City Council banned the group's stall in September, on the pretext that Salamanca was "a family market at which the presence of visible gays and lesbians is inappropriate".[18] Police were instructed to arrest anyone associated with the TGLRG, its stall, or any "visible" gay man or lesbian. Emphasis should be placed on the term "visible" for, as Rodney Croome has highlighted, hundreds of queer market-goers attended the Salamanca Market every week of the protest period without being arrested.

"The authorities were concerned not with same-sex preferences as such but with gays and lesbians being open about their sexuality,"[19] he wrote. The issue was not whether queer people were present at the market, but whether their sexuality was visible, and deemed threatening, to the heterosexual public. Gay people were tolerated in the 1980s if they behaved and presented like everybody else – straight, "normal". This was a time in which queer and trans Tasmanians were required to remain out of sight, because homosexuality was still commonly believed to be immoral, sinful and unnatural.

Like the women in Van Diemen's Land convict factories, queer people in the 1980s were othered and feared. Anti-gay groups such as Concerned

Residents Against Moral Pollution (CRAMP) and For a Caring Tasmania (FACT) allude to their need to "care" for Tasmania's social morality through their names, and were known to host large rallies with attendees chanting "kill them!"[20] Rodney Croome recalled politicians addressing such rallies and "calling for the reintroduction of the death penalty for homosexuality or calling for police to wipe us out".[21]

For the purpose of Tasmanian gothic, this could almost be considered a witch hunt. Supporters of the movement flocked to Hobart in the weeks of the Salamanca protest, and in the course of seven weeks 130 people were arrested before the council lifted the ban. The arrests extended beyond gay men and lesbians, with police arresting observers and other market stallholders who displayed the TGLRG's petition.[22] This event is recognised as the largest act of gay rights civil disobedience in Australian history, with the number of arrests surpassing those of Sydney's first Mardi Gras in 1978.[23]

The intention of TGLRG's stall was to gain public exposure and raise the group's profile, the council's ban providing this through the national media attention that was caused by the Salamanca Market protests. Rather than remain invisible, like Terry Castle's apparitional lesbian, queer men and women were targeted at Salamanca for bringing homosexual issues to public awareness. This was even more significant in a state which stubbornly wanted to keep queer people locked away in a dusty, rotting closet.

The AIDS crisis brought about another fear in Australia which was sometimes referred to as the "gay plague" in the early 1980s, as the queer community was regularly blamed for the spread of the disease.[24] In 1984 there were claims that gay men were deliberately contaminating the blood supply in Queensland, when three babies died after receiving infected blood. A tabloid newspaper headline read "Die, you deviate", expressing the sentiment of one of the children's father who believed the "murderer" of his child should "commit suicide if he feels as bad about his actions as we are led to believe".[25]

These sentiments could just as well have been expressed in Tasmania, where medical practitioner and spokesman for the Hobart Council, Alderman John Freeman, refused to support homosexual-rights demonstrations and stalls at a family market when what they were really talking about was "legitimising sodomy". With AIDS rampant, it was "hardly appropriate".[26] Associating AIDS exclusively with the queer community ostracised individuals and created a stigma that ultimately affected heterosexual men and women as well. Fear of the disease was consequently associated with queer men, creating all the more reason, in the eyes of a conservative public and state government, to maintain legal control over homosexual behaviour.

A QUEER GOTHIC LEGACY

Speaking to the Molesworth Committee in the late 1830s regarding convict transportation, William Ullathorne hinted of crimes "that, dare I describe them, would make your blood freeze, and your hair to rise erect in horror upon the pale flesh".[27] The subject of homosexuality and stories of "wretched men in depravity" were used in the mid-19th century by the anti-transportation movement who wanted an end to the convict penal system. In the colonial squattocracy, "deprave" acts that make one's hair stand on end were believed to be inappropriate for a civilised society. Homosexuality did not fade into nonexistence upon the end of convict transportation, when Van Diemen's Land became Tasmania, but continued to shock, unnerve, and repulse well into the twentieth century (and beyond).

Histories of homosexuality fit into what Jim Davidson described as the Tasmanian Gothic, by being branded as something to be repressed and controlled. Terminology such as homophobia and transphobia imply an inherent fear, something that is again prevalent in the gothic genre. Through deliberate acts of othering, condemning queer and trans people to feel inherently different and "wrong", a sense of displacement inevitably grows within the LGBTQI community. This becomes apparent in the Salamanca protest and broader campaign for law reform in the twentieth century, where State Premier Robin Gray stated in 1988 that homosexuals were "not welcome in Tasmania".[28] Laws that criminalised male homosexuality were considered, even in the late 20th century, as "necessary public safeguards" by members of Cabinet in Tasmania.[29] The implication being that laws were in place to "safeguard" non-queer people from the immorality caused by homosexuality.

Queer history is as important to Tasmania as the state's gothic aesthetic, and the two should be considered in relation to one another. While local support has increased, with Tasmania recording a higher approval rating for marriage equality in the 2017 postal vote than the national average,[30] the long history of discrimination and social isolation should continuously be acknowledged. *The Yellow Line* succeeds by literally shining a light, alongside messages of hope, at the location of Australia's largest act of queer civil disobedience. With this permanent installation, queer people for generations to come can read these lines of comfort in peace, not needing to fear imprisonment for their sexual identity. Here, too, they might feel a shiver run up their spine as a ghost of the past walks through them, collecting signatures on a petition that urges to be seen.

■ ■ ■

ENDNOTES

1. Greg Lehman, "Tasmanian gothic", *Griffith Review*, edition 39, January 2013.
2. Graham Willett, *Living Out Loud: A history of gay and lesbian activism in Australia* (Sydney: Allen & Unwin, 2000), 232.
3. Pauline Palmer, *The Queer Uncanny: New perspectives on the gothic* (Cardiff: University of Wales Press, 2012), 153.
4. Robert Hughes, *The Fatal Shore* (London: Vintage, 2003), 264.
5. Jim Davidson, "Tasmanian Gothic", *Meanjin* 48.2 (1989): 310.
6. Lehman, "Tasmanian gothic".
7. Briony Kidd, "How Tasmania became the gothic muse of Australian film and TV", *Guardian*, published November 24, 2016, https://www.theguardian.com/film/2016/nov/24/how-tasmania-became-the-gothic-muse-of-australian-film-and-tv.
8. Ibid.
9. Gays and Lesbians Aboriginal Alliance, "Peopling the Empty Mirror: The prospects for lesbian and gay Aboriginal history", in *Queer Perspectives II: More essays in Australian gay culture*, ed. Robert Aldrich (Sydney: Department of Economic History with the Australian Centre for Gay and Lesbian Research, University of Sydney, 1994), 17.
10. Terry Castle, *The Apparitional Lesbian: Female homosexuality and modern culture* (New York: Columbia University Press, 1993), 2.
11. Martha Vicinus, "Lesbian History: All theory and no facts or all facts and no theory?" *Radical History Review* 60 (1994): 66.
12. Robert Hughes described Cascades as "swarmed with lesbians", *The Fatal Shore*, 530.
13. "Female Factory – The Flash Mob", *Colonial Times*, March 10, 1840, 4, https://trove.nla.gov.au/newspaper/article/8750568.
14. Ibid.
15. Alexandra Purvis and Joseph Castellino, "A History of Homosexual Law Reform in Tasmania", *University of Tasmania Law Review* 16.1 (1997): 17-18.
16. Ibid., 19.

17. Nick Toonen, "Gay Law Reform Victory Achieved #2", October 2017, YouTube video, https://www.youtube.com/watch?v=ZqPmbccdBaA&list=PLse9LX4dNT0Un6ihrxm3MP4Hl1WIuyb0w&index=1.
18. Rodney Croome, "'Out and About': The public rights of lesbians and gays in Tasmania", *Australian Gay and Lesbian Law Journal* 2 (1992):, 64.
19. Ibid.
20. Ruby Grant, "Not going to the mainland: queer women's narratives of place in Tasmania, Australia", *Gender, Place & Culture*, 29 June 2020, 5.
21. Shalailah Medhora, "Gay sex was illegal in Tasmania until 1997. How did it turn itself around?", *Triple J Hack*, published November 15, 2018, https://www.abc.net.au/triplej/programs/hack/how-tasmania-turned-itself-around-on-lgbti-rights-same-sex-marr/10502304.
22. Willett, *Living Out Loud*, 232.
23. Ibid.
24. Frank Bongiorno, *The Eighties: The decade that transformed Australia* (Collingwood: Black Inc., 2015), 202.
25. Frank Bongiorno, *The Sex Lives of Australians: A history* (Collingwood: Black Inc., 2012), 278–279.
26. "Hobart getting used to bizarre protests", *Canberra Times*, December 14, 1988, 9, https://trove.nla.gov.au/newspaper/article/102037751
27. Hughes, *The Fatal Shore*, 266.
28. Grant, "Not going to the mainland", 5.
29. Croome, "Out and About", 66.
30. Grant, "Not going to the mainland", 6.

The mysterious journey of Captain Charles Bayley's scrimshaw cane

BRADLEY WOOD

On December 6, 1846, Captain Charles Bayley was in a desperate struggle for his life. The whaleboat he was in had capsized and the other five men who crewed it had all, one by one, slipped off and drowned. As the only one who couldn't swim, Captain Bayley had desperately maintained a grip onto the hull in the tossing sea by wedging a finger in the boat's drain hole, next to the keel. Battered and bruised, barely conscious in the frigid waters south of New Zealand, he struck out with his free arm to bat away the albatrosses that now descended on him. Ironically, the birds who had come to feed on the dying man would play a part in his deliverance.

Many Tasmanians would know of Captain Charles Bayley as "Hobart's most successful whaling captain and whaleship owner".[1] I knew a little about the Bayley family from my visit to their historic home Runnymede in the Hobart suburb of New Town, but developed a greater interest in their lives whilst undertaking research on scrimshaw walking canes in the State Library of Tasmania. While perusing Richard Malley's *Graven by the Fishermen Themselves*, I came across a photo of an exquisitely carved whale-bone cane in Mystic Seaport Museum in America. It was a very fine piece with "C BAYLEY" spelled out in carpenter's tacks around the hexagonal circumference beneath the top section of the cane.[2]

My immediate thought was, could this cane possibly have belonged to Captain Charles Bayley of Hobart Town? I had seen two whalebone canes that

The whalebone cane showing a portion of the lettering "C BAYLEY".
Louise Zarmati

belonged to Captain James Kelly, "father and founder" of whaling in Tasmania, on display in the Queen Victoria Museum in Launceston. High-quality scrimshaw canes like these were an insignia of the whaling industry and Charles Bayley would surely have owned at least one as well.

However, without presenting any reason apart from the shared name, Richard Malley suggested that the cane was carved around 1868 by an American sailor, also named Charles Bayley. If Malley was wrong, could this be a lost piece of Tasmanian history sitting unrecognised and unheralded in a far-off American museum? I decided to investigate and ended up on a journey of discovery that would ultimately take me across the world to Mystic, Connecticut.

Who was Captain Charles Bayley of Hobart Town, and how does his life or death dilemma in the frigid waters off the coast of New Zealand relate to the scrimshaw cane in the Mystic museum?

Charles Bayley was born in Essex in 1813 and left England at an early age for a life at sea. In 1827, aged only 14, he was working in the bay whaling industry in southern Tasmania.[3]

When Hobart was founded in its present location in 1804, it was impossible to miss the extraordinary number of southern right whales that visited the Derwent on their way north along the east coast between June and September. Reverend Knopwood noted in his journal on June 28, 1804, "This eve we heard a great many whales in the river very near us," and less than two weeks later the whaler *Alexander* "anchored in Sandy Bay near the East side of the river [Derwent] to take whales".[4]

When whales were plentiful during their winter migration, it was a relatively easy to station a lookout on shore and send out whaleboats to catch them as they swam past. Once caught, the enormous carcass was towed to shore for processing which involved the stinking and difficult task of stripping the whale and rendering its blubber to valuable oil.

Over the years, Bayley worked his way up through the ranks, gaining experience in both whaling and the inter-colonial trade between Van Diemen's Land, the coastal whaling stations and the new settlement at Port Phillip later known as Melbourne. By 1839 he was Chief Officer of the *Wallaby* under Captain Henry Wishart, a popular leader with whom Bayley had sailed for several years. Charles' brother James had also now emigrated to Hobart and joined him serving on board the same ship.[5]

But death is never far from such a dangerous occupation. On August 7, 1839, after a successful catch begun in April which nearly filled their hold with oil, Captain Wishart was killed chasing the last whale of the voyage. Wishart's whaleboat was flipped by the whale near Wilsons Promontory and tragically he was attacked by a shark while swimming to the nearby shore. It was Charles Bayley's melancholy duty to "place his body in a tight-made case, filled with spirits" and return it to Hobart for burial.[6]

Bayley was dismayed but not deterred by Wishart's grisly demise and it also gave him his first taste of command, standing in for his captain. A later photographic portrait of Charles Bayley gives the impression of a man who would not be easily daunted. With a high forehead and a swathe of dark beard encircling a prominent jaw, Bayley looks the very picture of stern authority. But the lack of a moustache opens his face, revealing what his contemporaries saw as "unflinching integrity and honesty of purpose".[7]

The death of Captain Wishart also occurred at a turning point for the whaling industry. The unsustainable, indiscriminate slaughter of the Southern Right whale led to an inevitable and drastic decline in the numbers of that species. 1841 marked the peak year for their capture in Tasmanian waters; after this a new strategy was needed to fill the ships casks with oil.[8] Sperm whales, which "had been reduced but not obliterated by the ceaseless hunting", were now the most desirable catch, and Bayley would sail to whaling grounds farther afield where sperm whales could be hunted.[9]

The artefact storage facility at Mystic Seaport Museum.
Louise Zarmati

Sperm whales are larger than the southern right, and were a more a profitable catch because they had "the best oil available for lighting and for lubricating fine machinery".[10] They also frequented the open ocean so the business of catching them was longer, harder and more dangerous work.

The sperm whale is a toothed whale, with a long, straight lower jaw and a line of pointed, peg-like teeth that fit in corresponding sockets in the upper jaw when closed. These teeth and jawbones were prized by sailors as material for crafting and carving objects during their leisure hours. The functional or decorative items, known as scrimshaw, were either for personal use, or sale to the public at harbour markets. Charles' younger brother James became a well-known exponent of the art.

In May 2019, I travelled to Mystic Seaport Museum in Connecticut to examine the Bayley cane. It had been made from a section of the great lower jaw of a sperm whale. Once a whale was cut up, "the great jaw-pans were sawn off and placed at the disposal of anybody who wanted pieces of bone for "scrimshaw", or carved work".[11]

Being the one long straight bone of the sperm whale, the jaw was ideal for making walking sticks and the teeth could be carved into cane handles, like the carved Turk's Head rope knot that adorns the top of the Bayley cane. The cane also has an unusually elaborate design along its length with a section of four separated columns, another of joined columns and several sections of traditional hatching and spiralling rope motifs. The joined columns are remarkably similar to a cane in the Runnymede collection made by James Bayley.

In order to determine the ownership of the scrimshaw cane, it is also necessary to examine the career of the American sailor, Charles Bayley. Due to the exceptional quality of craftsmanship of the cane, it is not unreasonable to expect that it was an experienced whaler and scrimshander who produced such beautiful work. Instead, the American Charles Bayley is recorded as having had only one whaling voyage from 1868–1871 out of New Bedford on the *Roman*.[12]

In the 19th century, canes functioned as decorative fashion items – a gentleman's accessory advertising their wealth and authority. Sailors made and sold them for extra income, but it would be out of place with their social status if they were to keep and carry one. It is also strange that a relatively low status whaler like the American Charles Bayley would put his own name on it and make it unsellable. This leads me to conclude that cane was probably not made by this Charles Bayley.

Back in Van Diemen's Land, and several whaling voyages later, Captain Charles Bayley had been appointed master of the whaling ship *Fortitude*. He was also sufficiently ambitious and wealthy to back his luck in April 1846 and buy a quarter share in the ship. This was a step up in respectability and social status for Charles, so it would not be surprising if his brother James decided to mark the occasion with the gift of a scrimshaw cane marked with his name.[13]

At the Bayleys' luxurious home, "Runnymede", there is a significant collection of scrimshaw carved items, including a number of very handsome canes. Many of these were made by James Bayley after the 1860s when he was captaining his own whaling voyages, on which he is said to have taken on board a lathe to help with his part-time carpentry.[14] In 1846, though James Bayley was still only 22 years old, he had been whaling with Charles for six years, more than enough time to develop the interest and ability to make a beautiful whalebone cane as a memento for his brother, something emblematic of their trade.

At this point in my research, I felt reasonably convinced that the cane in the Mystic Seaport Museum had been made by James Bayley and owned by Charles Bayley. The only missing link was how it may have travelled from a Hobart whaling captain to a museum in Connecticut. But the American connection is not too hard to envisage, because America was the dominant whaling nation at this time. The American whaling fleet of 1844 "consisted of 675 vessels, and most of these were in the Pacific Ocean,"[15] compared with the 25 colonial ships engaged in whaling at the time.[16]

On Good Friday 1847, the majority of the 47 whaling ships then anchored off Hobart were American.[17] This cluster of foreign whalers in the Derwent was a result of the local attitude that the ships of other nations were not so much competitors as customers. Their repair and refitting in the port were encouraged in 1845 by exempting them from port dues. There would have been rivalry, but probably also a type of hunters' camaraderie between the various whaling vessels. When these ships encountered each other at sea, having been away from their home port for months or even longer, they would happily exchange news and assist each other.

Amongst these vessels in the southern waters was the American whaling ship *Factor*, whose master was Captain Shubael Hawes. Hawes was born in New Bedford, Massachusetts, which had been settled by the Puritan pilgrims from England in the 17th century, so fittingly his first name Shubael means "captive of God". Captain Hawes was tall for his era with dark hair, light skin, and a reputation for being "warm-hearted and generous" with his crews. In 1846, at the time of Captain Bayley's struggle to survive in his overturned whaleboat, Captain Hawes was 44 years old and widely respected as an experienced and skilled mariner.[18]

On December 5, 1846, the day before Captain Bayley had come to grief, the *Fortitude*'s lookout had sighted a large sperm whale in the water south of New Zealand and three whale-boats had been lowered to chase it, Captain Bayley amongst them.[19] It was not unusual for the Captain to be directly and actively involved in the pursuit. American seaman Charles Tyng wrote in his memoir that a whaling boat's crew consisted of "six: four sailors to row, an experienced steersman and a harpoon man, which is the captain or one of the mates".[20]

Five kilometres from the ship, Bayley and his men secured the whale, but night came on with gales and heavy seas, while the whaleboats and crews clung to the whale until daylight. At dawn, and still battling rough seas, Bayley sighted the ship. Leaving the other two boats and crews still tethered to the whale, they struck out in his whaleboat towards the *Fortitude* but their boat capsized only 300 metres distant. Quickly the freezing water claimed all on board except Bayley, who survived by the clinging to the upturned whaleboat.

Eventually Bayley's drifting whaleboat and battered body were located by the *Fortitude*'s crew when they sighted and followed the flight of albatrosses that were menacing him. Bayley's finger had become so swollen and thoroughly wedged in the hole that they had to split the plank it was in with a tomahawk before he could be brought on board, more dead than alive.

The *Fortitude* had no doctor, so they sailed to the shelter of Paterson Inlet on Stewart Island in hope of finding medical aid. The ship's log for December 7, 1846 reads "Captain very bad … Came into Patterson River in company with the American ship *Factor* [of New Bedford] … Got the doctor of the ship to attend the Captain."[21]

The *Factor*'s surgeon, a man by the name of Arch Fennaut, who had been taken on board the *Factor* in Sydney on September 14, 1846, attended Captain Bayley and he recovered remarkably quickly. Fennaut would later be discharged by the *Factor* back in Sydney on February 17, 1847.[22]

No doubt but for the *Fortitude*'s timely encounter with the *Factor*, and the assistance rendered by Captain Hawes and his surgeon, Charles Bayley would certainly have perished. The two ships encountered each other at sea again on two more occasions: December 26, 1846, and January 11, 1847. By this time Charles Bayley was well recovered. I think it probable that Captain Charles Bayley showed his appreciation to Captain Hawes for saving his life by gifting him his personal walking stick at one of these meetings.

Captain Bayley would continue whaling for another decade before settling into more diverse business interests and becoming a beloved and respected Hobart citizen. Of his death on January 20, 1875, the *Hobart Mercury* wrote that, "he took a formal leave of his friends, and departed as if proceeding on an ordinary journey. Death had no terrors for him, and when he passed away, he left few peers in his walk of life."

Captain Hawes returned to America to try farming and gold mining before going back to the sea and journeying to Calcutta where he died in 1856. His gravestone lies in a New Bedford cemetery, about 125 kilometres from Mystic.[23]

In 1941 Mystic Seaport Museum acquired the *Charles W. Morgan*, an American whaling ship built in New Bedford in 1841. The ship had been part of a private exhibition since 1926 at Colonel Edward H. R. Green's Round Hill estate in South Dartmouth close to New Bedford. It is the only preserved 19th century whaling ship in the world. When it arrived in Mystic, it came with an assortment of items from the exhibition, and part of the "job lot" was a

The whaling vessel *Charles W. Morgan*, preserved at the Mystic Seaport Museum in Mystic, Connecticut.
Louise Zarmati

beautifully carved whale-bone walking stick with no tags or description other than the name "C BAYLEY" spelled out in tiny nails.

In 2019, I was visiting the US and arranged to see the Bayley cane in Mystic Seaport Museum. The open-air museum is built like a small village port around the major exhibit, the *Charles W. Morgan*, the last old sail whaling vessel. The cane is not on exhibit but held in the museum's repository. I gently held Charles Bayley's scrimshaw cane in my hands and marvelled at its delicately carved details. I then told the staff the story of where I believe the Bayley cane came from, and how it came to be in their museum, a symbol of co-operation between a vibrant new northern continent and an even newer southern one.

∎ ∎ ∎

ENDNOTES

1. Rhys Richards, *Captain Charles Bayley: Whaling Master 1813–1875*, ed. Graeme Broxam (Hobart: Navarine Publishing, 2019), 1.
2. Richard C. Malley, *Graven by the Fishermen Themselves: Scrimshaw in Mystic Seaport Museum* (Mystic, CT: The Museum, 1983), 91–92.
3. Richards, *Captain Charles Bayley*, 4.
4. Mary Nicholls, *The Diary of the Reverend Robert Knopwood, 1803–1838: First Chaplain of Van Diemen's Land* (Hobart: Tasmanian Historical Research Association, 1977), 55, 59.
5. Peter Mercer, *A Most Dangerous Occupation: Whaling, whalers and the Bayleys: Runnymede's maritime heritage*. (Hobart: Runnymede Committee, National Trust of Australia, 2002), 47.
6. *Colonial Times*. "Shipping Intelligence", April 9, 1839. http://nla.gov.au/nla.news-article8749567, accessed September 18, 2020.
7. "Charles Bayley, (1813–1875)", Obituaries Australia, National Centre of Biography, Australian National University, http://oa.anu.edu.au/obituary/bayley-charles-13656/text24426, accessed 19 September 2020.
8. Graeme Broxam, Dale Chatwin, and Rhys Richards, "The Scale of Tasmanian Sail Whaling: Establishing base lines and global comparisons," *Papers of the Hobart Whaling Conference: May 6–7, 2019*, 65. (Hobart: Navarine Publishing, 2020).
9. Geoffrey Blainey, *The Tyranny of Distance: How distance shaped Australia's history*, (Melbourne, Victoria: Sun Books Macmillan, 1982), 113.
10. Mercer, *A Most Dangerous Occupation*, 1–2.
11. Frank T. Bullen, *The Cruise of the "Cachalot": Round the world after sperm whales*, (London: Smith, Elder & Co., 1912), 82.
12. "Roman: 1868–1871", Whaling History. https://whalinghistory.org/?s=AC124751, accessed September 18, 2020.
13. Richards, *Captain Charles Bayley*, 9.
14. Mercer, *A Most Dangerous Occupation*, 63.
15. William J. Dakin, *Whalemen Adventurers*, (Sydney: Angus & Robertson, 1934), 69.
16. Dale Chatwin, and Graeme Broxam, "The Popular Picture of Tasmanian Whaling: Fact or Fantasy?", *Papers of the Hobart Whaling Conference: May 6–7, 2019*, (Hobart: Navarine Publishing, 2020), 83.
17. Blainey, *The Tyranny of Distance*, 113.
18. "Captain Shubael Hawes III (1802–1856)", Find a Grave, https://www.findagrave.com/memorial/92248977/shubael-hawes, accessed September 20, 2020.
19. "Domestic Intelligence." *Colonial Times*. February 9, 1847, http://nla.gov.au/nla.news-article8760048.
20. Charles Tyng, *Before the Wind: The memoir of an American sea captain, 1808–1833*, ed. Susan Fels, (New York, NY: Penguin Books, 2000), 82.

21. Richards, *Captain Charles Bayley*, 15–16.
22. "Factor: 1844–1847", Whaling History, https:// https://whalinghistory.org/?s=AV04793, accessed September 21, 2020.
23. Find a Grave website, https://www.findagrave.com/memorial/92248977/shubael-hawes, accessed 30 August 2019.

www.ingramcontent.com/pod-product-compliance
Lightning Source LLC
Chambersburg PA
CBHW061807290426
44109CB00031B/2959